SMOOTHIES
& JUICES

SMOOTHIES & JUICES

DELICIOUS DRINKS, BLENDS, TONICS, SHAKES
AND FLOATS: MORE THAN 150 IRRESISTIBLE RECIPES
SHOWN IN OVER 250 STUNNING PHOTOGRAPHS

Suzannah Olivier and Joanna Farrow

LORENZ BOOKS

This edition is published by Lorenz Books,
an imprint of Anness Publishing Ltd,
Hermes House,
88–89 Blackfriars Road,
London SE1 8HA
tel. 020 7401 2077; fax 020 7633 9499

www.lorenzbooks.com; www.annesspublishing.com

If you like the images in this book and would like
to investigate using them for publishing, promotions
or advertising, please visit our website
www.practicalpictures.com for more information.

UK agent: The Manning Partnership Ltd;
tel. 01225 478444; fax 01225 478440;
sales@manning-partnership.co.uk
UK distributor: Grantham Book Services Ltd;
tel. 01476 541080; fax 01476 541061;
orders@gbs.tbs-ltd.co.uk
North American agent/distributor: National Book
Network; tel. 301 459 3366; fax 301 429 5746;
www.nbnbooks.com
Australian agent/distributor: Pan Macmillan Australia;
tel. 1300 135 113; fax 1300 135 103;
customer.service@macmillan.com.au
New Zealand agent/distributor: David Bateman Ltd;
tel. (09) 415 7664; fax (09) 415 8892

Publisher: Joanna Lorenz
Senior Managing Editor: Conor Kilgallon
Recipes: Suzannah Olivier and Joanna Farrow
Photography: Gus Filgate and Craig Robertson,
with additional pictures by Janine Hosegood and
Simon Smith
Production Controller: Don Campaniello
Editor: Brian Burns
Designer: Nigel Partridge

ETHICAL TRADING POLICY
At Anness Publishing we believe that business should be
conducted in an ethical and ecologically sustainable
way, with respect for the environment and a proper
regard to the replacement of the natural resources
we employ.

As a publisher, we use a lot of wood pulp to make
high-quality paper for printing, and that wood
commonly comes from spruce trees. We are therefore
currently growing more than 500,000 trees in two
Scottish forest plantations near Aberdeen – Berrymoss
(130 hectares/320 acres) and West Touxhill (125
hectares/305 acres). The forests we manage contain
twice the number of trees employed each year in
paper-making for our books.

Because of this ongoing ecological investment
programme, you, as our customer, can have the pleasure
and reassurance of knowing that a tree is being
cultivated on your behalf to naturally replace the
materials used to make the book you are holding.
Our forestry programme is run in accordance with the
UK Woodland Assurance Scheme (UKWAS) and will be
certified by the internationally recognized Forest
Stewardship Council (FSC). The FSC is a non-
government organization dedicated to promoting
responsible management of the world's forests.
Certification ensures forests are managed in an
environmentally sustainable and socially responsible
basis. For further information about this scheme, go to
www.annesspublishing.com/trees

A CIP catalogue record for this book is available from
the British Library.

NOTES
For all recipes, quantities are given in both metric
and imperial measures and, where appropriate, in
standard cups and spoons.
Follow one set of measures, but not a mixture,
because they are not interchangeable.

Standard spoon and cup measures are level.
1 tsp = 5ml, 1 tbsp = 15ml, 1 cup = 250ml/8fl oz.
Australian standard tablespoons are 20ml.
Australian readers should use 3 tsp in place of
1 tbsp for measuring small quantities.
American pints are 16fl oz/2 cups. American
readers should use 20fl oz/2.5 cups in place of
1 pint when measuring liquids.

Electric oven temperatures in this book are
for conventional ovens. When using a fan oven,
the temperature will probably need to be
reduced by about 10–20°C/20–40°F. Since ovens
vary, you should check with your manufacturer's
instruction book for guidance.

The nutritional analysis given for each recipe
is calculated per portion (i.e. serving or item),
unless otherwise stated. If the recipe gives a
range, such as Serves 4–6, then the nutritional
analysis will be for the smaller portion size, i.e.
6 servings. Measurements for sodium do not
include salt added to taste.

Medium (US large) eggs are used unless
otherwise stated.

Front cover shows Raspberry and oatmeal
smoothie – for recipe, see page 78.

Contents

Introduction

Juices, smoothies, shakes and blends fit neatly into hectic modern lives, enabling you to incorporate healthy habits into everyday routines. They are easy to make, convenient, delicious and packed with rejuvenating, healing and revitalizing nutrients.

THE BENEFITS OF JUICING

Freshly made juices are a potent source of nutrients. If you drink juices or blends on a regular basis, you'll enjoy clearer skin, better energy levels and balanced overall health. The antioxidants found in fruits and vegetables work most effectively when they are consumed together, and juicing encourages precisely this.

The healing power of certain foods was even recognized by no less a person than Hippocrates, who said: "Let food be your medicine."

Combining juices can emphasize particular flavours or effects in the same way that you would in cooking – sweet and sour, savoury and spicy, warming or cooling. But you can be more adventurous than you might be with conventionally prepared foods. The juice of fruits or vegetables often tastes much better than when they have been cooked or served raw. For instance, combine celery juice with pear and ginger and you get a complex, utterly delicious taste sensation.

Preparing juices and blends also has a psychological benefit. The very act of making them can make you feel good – you will feel you are nurturing and pampering yourself – and in addition, by using lots of fresh natural ingredients you will boost your own health and the health of your family. Juices and smoothies are great fun to make and to share: encourage your children to invent concoctions and join in the preparation, or share a juice instead of coffee with a friend.

THE HISTORY OF JUICING AND BLENDING

As long ago as the 19th century, doctors and naturopaths were using fresh fruit and vegetable juices to improve the health of their patients. People such as Dr Kellogg, Father Kniepp, Dr Max Bircher-Bener and Dr Max Gerson all helped to popularize the notion of the "juice cure".

LEFT: *Raspberry and apple, coconut and hazelnut are just two of many irresistible, health-giving fruit and nut blends.*

ABOVE: *Lavender and orange combine to make a perfect summer evening's drink.*

ABOVE: *Wheatgrass is a concentrated source of chlorophyll, which aids fatigue.*

ABOVE: *Cranberries and redcurrants make a vitamin-packed refresher.*

However, there is evidence to suggest that juicing is even older than this in the ancient practices of wine and scrumpy (apple cider) making. After extracting the fresh fruit juices, fermenting them into alcohol was simply a way of preserving the raw ingredients – and in those days it was safer to drink alcohol than drink water, which was often contaminated.

The modern concept of blending drinks and making smoothies probably began with mixed drinks such as cocktails. For the more virtuous and health-conscious among us, however, non-alcoholic juices and blends have always sat comfortably alongside the bar choice.

JUICING FOR HEALTH

Today, reliance on prepared and fast foods is increasingly giving way to a renewed interest in healthy eating. We've all heard that we should eat five portions of fruit and vegetables every day. One convenient way of achieving this is to embrace health drinks as easy-to-make snacks, quick breakfasts and fast energy boosters. Modern blenders, food processors and juicers make preparing them quick and easy.

In recent years – in an echo of those pioneering health enthusiasts – we have become more and more interested in natural ways of improving our health. In addition to

their more general health-boosting properties, juices and blends are also used for specific cleansing and detoxing, to speed recovery from illness and delay ageing. There are also those who maintain that juices can help prevent some cancers, although this has yet to be proven. Nevertheless, freshly made fruit and vegetable juices provide many of the essential vitamins and minerals that are vital for a healthy life.

It is not often that something so healthy also tastes so good and is a pleasure to incorporate into daily life. Perhaps this is why juices, blended drinks, smoothies and shakes are standing the test of time.

Super healthy juices

This chapter contains a selection of fabulous juices that have wonderful health benefits. Highly nutritious, natural additives such as wheatgrass, sprouting beans, echinacea and kelp are combined with everyday fruit and vegetables to make a range of feel-good juices for the seriously health conscious.

Parsnip pep

Although parsnips yield a relatively small amount of juice, the juicer produces an amazingly thick, sweet and creamy drink, perfect for adding body to any raw fruit and vegetable blend. Refreshing fennel, apple and pear are the perfect foils for the intense sweetness of parsnip and together produce the most tantalizing power-pack of a fresh juice.

MAKES 2 SMALL GLASSES

115g/4oz fennel
200g/7oz parsnips
1 apple
1 pear
a small handful of flat leaf parsley
crushed ice

1 Using a sharp knife, cut the fennel and parsnips into large similar-sized chunks. Quarter the apple and pear, carefully removing the core, if you like, then cut the quartered pieces in half.

2 Push half the prepared fruit and vegetables through a juicer, then follow with the parsley and the remaining fruit and vegetables.

3 Fill the glasses with ice and pour the juice over. Serve immediately.

Nutritional information per portion: Energy 113kcal/477kJ; Protein 2.7g; Carbohydrate 24g, of which sugars 17.2g; Fat 1.3g, of which saturates 0.2g; Cholesterol 0mg; Calcium 65mg; Fibre 2.2g; Sodium 19mg.

Clean sweep

This juice is so packed with goodness, you can almost feel it cleansing and detoxing your body. As well as valuable vitamins, the carrots and grapes provide plenty of natural sweetness, which blends perfectly with the mild pepperiness of the celery and fresh scent of parsley. Drink this juice on a regular basis to give your system a thorough clean-out.

MAKES 1 LARGE OR 2 SMALL GLASSES

1 celery stick
300g/11oz carrots
150g/5oz green grapes
several large sprigs of parsley
celery or carrot sticks, to serve

1 Using a sharp knife, roughly chop the celery and carrots. Push half of the celery, carrots and grapes through a juicer, then add the parsley sprigs. Add the remaining celery, carrots and grapes in the same way and juice until thoroughly combined.

2 Pour into one or two glasses and serve with celery or carrot stick stirrers.

Nutritional information per portion: Energy 99kcal/417kJ; Protein 1.3g; Carbohydrate 23.6g, of which sugars 22.8g; Fat 0.6g, of which saturates 0.2g; Cholesterol 0mg; Calcium 54mg; Fibre 1.3g; Sodium 48mg.

Broccoli booster

Hailed as a cure-all superfood and a vital ingredient in a healthy diet, broccoli's strong taste does, however, need a bit of toning down when juiced. Sweet and tangy apples and lemon juice soften its flavour, making a drink that's thoroughly enjoyable.

MAKES 1 LARGE GLASS

125g/4¼oz broccoli florets
2 eating apples
15ml/1 tbsp lemon juice
ice cubes

1 Cut the broccoli florets into small pieces and chop the apples.

2 Push both through a juicer and stir in the lemon juice. Serve in a tall glass with plenty of ice.

COOK'S TIP
Don't use the tough broccoli stalks as they provide little juice and don't have as good a flavour as the delicate florets. Broccoli is packed with antiviral and antibacterial nutrients and contains almost as much calcium as milk. It is also thought to prevent some cancers, so this juice is definitely worth drinking for its health benefits as well as its wonderful flavour.

Nutritional information per portion: Energy 111kcal/475kJ; Protein 6.1g; Carbohydrate 20.1g, of which sugars 19.7g; Fat 1.3g, of which saturates 0.3g; Cholesterol 0mg; Calcium 78mg; Fibre 6.5g; Sodium 14mg.

Wheatgrass tonic

Wheatgrass has many nutritional benefits. It is a concentrated source of chlorophyll, an energy booster, and also provides enzymes, vitamins and minerals. It has a distinctive flavour, so in this juice it is blended with mild white cabbage, but it is just as tasty combined with other vegetables.

MAKES 1 SMALL GLASS

50g/2oz white cabbage
90g/3¹/₂oz wheatgrass

1 Using a small, sharp knife, roughly shred the cabbage.

2 Push through a juicer with the wheatgrass. Pour the juice into a small glass and serve immediately.

Nutritional information per portion: Energy 36kcal/149kJ; Protein 3.2g; Carbohydrate 3.9g, of which sugars 3.8g; Fat 0.8g, of which saturates 0.1g; Cholesterol 0mg; Calcium 178mg; Fibre 1.9g; Sodium 130mg.

Iron crazy

This energizing drink contains spinach, apricots, carrots and pumpkin seeds – all rich in iron – as well as kelp, a type of seaweed, for an invigorating lift. As iron is essential for carrying oxygen in the blood, a shortage can quickly lead to tiredness and anaemia.

MAKES 1 SMALL GLASS

50g/2oz/¹/₄ cup ready-to-eat dried apricots
15ml/1 tbsp pumpkin seeds
250g/9oz carrots
50g/2oz spinach
15ml/1 tbsp lemon juice
10ml/2 tsp kelp powder
mineral water
spinach leaf and pumpkin seeds, to decorate

1 Chop the apricots finely, cover with 100ml/3¹/₂ fl oz/ scant ¹/₂ cup boiling water and leave for 10 minutes.

2 Using a large, sharp knife, carefully chop the pumpkin seeds into small pieces. (Take it slowly at first as the whole seeds have a tendency to scatter.) Roughly chop the carrots.

3 Drain the apricots. Push the spinach through a juicer, followed by the apricots and carrots. Stir in the lemon juice, pumpkin seeds and kelp powder.

4 Pour the juice into a glass, top up with a little mineral water, decorate with a spinach leaf and pumpkin seeds, then serve immediately for maximum benefit.

Nutritional information per portion: Energy 266kcal/1115kJ; Protein 7.9g; Carbohydrate 41.6g, of which sugars 37.8g; Fat 8.6g, of which saturates 1g; Cholesterol 0mg; Calcium 201mg; Fibre 4.1g; Sodium 140mg.

Body builder

Wheatgerm is packed with vitamins B and E , protein and minerals. Combined with bananas, and boosted with orange juice and linseeds, it makes a carbohydrate-rich drink that is perfect before exercise. The essential fatty acids in linseeds are good for the heart.

MAKES 1 LARGE GLASS

30ml/2 tbsp wheatgerm
1 large banana, chopped
130g/4¹/₂ oz/generous ¹/₂ cup soya yogurt
15ml/1 tbsp linseeds (flax seeds)
juice of 1 lime
juice of 1 large orange
mineral water (optional)
linseeds and grated lime zest, to decorate

1 Put the wheatgerm, two-thirds of the banana, the yogurt and linseeds in a blender or food processor. Blend until smooth then, using a plastic spatula or spoon, scrape down the side of the bowl if necessary. Stir well.

2 Add the lime and orange juice to the yogurt mixture and blend again until evenly mixed. Pour the juice into a large glass and top up with mineral water. Decorate with linseeds, lime zest and the remaining banana, then serve.

COOK'S TIP
Brewer's yeast is another healthy supplement that can be added to energy-boosting drinks. Rich in B vitamins and minerals, it is great for increasing vitality.

Nutritional information per portion: Energy 384kcal/1619kJ; Protein 18.4g; Carbohydrate 41.6g, of which sugars 31.1g; Fat 14.1g, of which saturates 2.5g; Cholesterol 3mg; Calcium 127mg; Fibre 4.8g; Sodium 10mg.

Red alert

This juice is perfect for those times when you're not thinking straight or you need to concentrate. Beetroot, carrots and spinach all contain folic acid, which is known to help maintain a healthy brain, while the addition of fresh orange juice will give your body a natural vitamin charge. This delicious and vibrant blend is guaranteed to set your tastebuds tingling.

MAKES 1 LARGE OR 2 SMALL GLASSES

200g/7oz raw beetroot (beets)
1 carrot
1 large orange
50g/2oz spinach

1 Using a sharp knife, cut the beetroot into wedges. Roughly chop the carrot, then cut away the skin from the orange and roughly slice the flesh.

2 Push the orange, beetroot – and use fresh beetroot only – and carrot pieces alternately through a juicer, then add the spinach. Pour into glasses.

Nutritional information per portion: Energy 65kcal/273kJ; Protein 2.8g; Carbohydrate 13.2g, of which sugars 12.4g; Fat 0.5g, of which saturates 0.1g; Cholesterol 0mg; Calcium 75mg; Fibre 1.4g; Sodium 113mg.

Veggie boost

This simple blend makes a great juice boost. It has pure clean flavours and a chilli kick that is guaranteed to revitalize flagging energy levels. Tomatoes and carrots are rich in the valuable antioxidant betacarotene, which is reputed to fight cancer, and they contain a good supply of vitamins A, C and E, all of which are essential for good health.

MAKES 2 GLASSES

3 tomatoes
1 fresh red or green chilli
250g/9oz carrots
juice of 1 orange
crushed ice

1 Quarter the tomatoes and roughly chop the chilli. (If you prefer a milder juice, remove the seeds and white pith from the chilli before chopping.) Scrub the carrots and chop them roughly.

2 Push the carrots through a juicer, then follow with the tomatoes and chilli. Add the orange juice and stir well to mix. Fill two tumblers with crushed ice, pour the juice over and serve.

Nutritional information per portion: Energy 84kcal/351kJ; Protein 2.7g; Carbohydrate 16.9g, of which sugars 16.3g; Fat 1g, of which saturates 0.3g; Cholesterol 0mg; Calcium 52mg; Fibre 4.6g; Sodium 49mg.

Immune zoom

Red- and orange-coloured fruits and vegetables, and the herb echinacea, are particularly good for protecting against, or fighting off, colds or flu. Rich with powerful antioxidants, they also protect against many more serious illnesses.

MAKES 2 GLASSES

1 small mango
1 eating apple
2 passion fruit
juice of 1 orange
5ml/1 tsp echinacea
mineral water (optional)
ice cubes (optional)

1 Halve the mango, cutting down one side of the flat stone (pit). Remove the stone and scoop the flesh from the skin. Roughly chop the flesh and place in a blender or food processor.

2 Peel, core and roughly chop the apple. Add to the blender and process together until smooth, scraping the mixture down from the side of the bowl, if necessary.

3 Halve the passion fruit and scoop the pulp into the mango and apple purée. Add the orange juice and echinacea, then blend briefly.

4 Thin with a little mineral water, if you like, pour into two glasses and serve. Otherwise, transfer the juice into a jug (pitcher) and chill in the refrigerator, then serve in large glasses with ice cubes and slices of mango to decorate.

Nutritional information per portion: Energy 69kcal/296kJ; Protein 1.2g; Carbohydrate 16.7g, of which sugars 16.4g; Fat 0.3g, of which saturates 0.1g; Cholesterol 0mg; Calcium 15mg; Fibre 0.5g; Sodium 8mg.

Ginseng juice

This vibrantly coloured, deliciously tangy juice is also an excellent boost for the immune system. Ginseng is a natural cure-all that is claimed to stimulate digestion, reduce tiredness, alleviate stress, strengthen the immune system and revive a flagging libido.

MAKES 1 GLASS

1 red or orange (bell) pepper
200g/7oz pumpkin
1 large apricot
squeeze of lemon juice
5ml/1 tsp ginseng powder
ice cubes

1 Using a sharp knife, discard the core from the pepper and roughly chop the flesh. Slice the pumpkin in half. Scoop out the pips (seeds) with a spoon and then cut away the skin. Chop the flesh. Halve and stone (pit) the apricot.

2 Push the pumpkin, pepper and apricot pieces through a juicer. Add a squeeze of lemon juice and the ginseng powder, and stir well to mix together. Pour the juice over ice cubes in a tall glass and serve.

COOK'S TIP
If you are suffering from a cold or flu, or can sense its imminent arrival, echinacea can be taken in about 5ml/1 tsp servings, which can be repeated throughout the day. Check the recommended dosage on the manufacturer's packaging before use, however.

Nutritional information per portion: Energy 94kcal/398kJ; Protein 3.5g; Carbohydrate 18.5g, of which sugars 17g; Fat 1.1g, of which saturates 0.4g; Cholesterol 0mg; Calcium 78mg; Fibre 5.5g; Sodium 8mg.

Ginger juice

Fresh root ginger is one of the best natural cures for indigestion and it helps to settle upset stomachs, whether caused by food poisoning or motion sickness. In this unusual fruity blend, it is simply mixed with fresh, juicy pineapple and sweet-tasting carrot, creating a quick and easy remedy that can be juiced up in minutes – and tastes delicious too.

MAKES 1 GLASS

½ small pineapple
25g/1oz fresh root ginger
1 carrot
ice cubes

1 Using a sharp knife, cut away the skin from the pineapple, then halve and remove the core. Roughly slice the pineapple flesh. Peel and roughly chop the ginger, then chop the carrot.

2 Push the carrot, ginger and pineapple through a juicer and pour into a glass. Add ice cubes and serve immediately.

Nutritional information per portion: Energy 108kcal/461kJ; Protein 1.3g; Carbohydrate 26.1g, of which sugars 25.8g; Fat 0.6g, of which saturates 0.1g; Cholesterol 0mg; Calcium 55mg; Fibre 4.2g; Sodium 23mg.

Sleep easy

Some herbal teas are known for their purely soporific qualities, but this concoction is slightly more substantial – the last thing you want is to go to bed hungry. Blended bananas provide slow-release carbohydrates to sustain you through the night and lettuce is renowned for its sleep-inducing properties. It's just what you need when you want to relax.

MAKES 1 LARGE GLASS

1 chamomile teabag
90g/3¹/₂oz iceberg lettuce
1 small banana
juice of ¹/₂ lemon

1 Cover the teabag with 150ml/¹/₄ pint/²/₃ cup boiling water and leave to steep for 10 minutes. Meanwhile, chop the lettuce. Drain the teabag.

2 Chop the banana into a blender or food processor, add the lettuce and blend well until smooth, scraping the mixture down from the sides of the bowl, if necessary. Add the lemon juice and chamomile tea and blend briefly until smooth. Serve immediately.

Nutritional information per portion: Energy 89kcal/376kJ; Protein 1.7g; Carbohydrate 20.1g, of which sugars 18.3g; Fat 0.7g, of which saturates 0.2g; Cholesterol 0mg; Calcium 30mg; Fibre 1.7g; Sodium 4mg.

Mixed salad

Despite their reputation as being full of water, lettuce and cucumber contain important minerals such as calcium and zinc, alongside other crucial nutrients like vitamin K. Spinach contains plenty of betacarotene and has cancer-fighting properties. Juiced with ripe pears for maximum sweetness, a regular dose of this super juice can only enhance your health.

MAKES 2–3 GLASSES

½ cucumber

½ iceberg, cos or romaine lettuce

2 large, ripe pears

75g/3oz fresh spinach

6–8 radishes

crushed ice

sliced radishes and cucumber, to decorate

1 Using a small, sharp knife, chop the cucumber into chunks. Roughly tear the lettuce into pieces. Quarter the pears and remove the core.

2 Push all the ingredients through a juicer. Pour over crushed ice in tall glasses and serve with sliced radishes and cucumber swizzle sticks.

COOK'S TIP

Although it can taste fairly bland in a salad, unpeeled cucumber has a surprisingly intense flavour when it is juiced. If you prefer a lighter taste, peel the cucumber with a sharp knife before juicing.

Nutritional information per portion: Energy 64kcal/270kJ; Protein 2.1g; Carbohydrate 12.9g, of which sugars 12.8g; Fat 0.7g, of which saturates 0.1g; Cholesterol 0mg; Calcium 88mg; Fibre 3.9g; Sodium 44mg.

Bright eyes

Thin-skinned citrus fruits like clementines can be put through the juicer without peeling, adding a zesty kick to the final mix – and saving time when you're in a hurry. This vibrant, intensely flavoured carrot and clementine combination is packed with vitamin A, which is essential for healthy vision, and vitamin C to give an extra boost to the whole system.

MAKES 2 GLASSES

200g/7oz carrots
**6 clementines, plus extra wedges or slices
    to decorate**
ice cubes

1 Scrub the carrots and, using a sharp knife, chop them into large chunks of a similar size. Quarter the clementines, discarding any pips (seeds).

2 Push the clementine quarters through a juicer, then repeat the procedure with the carrot chunks.

3 Pour the juice over ice cubes in tall glasses and decorate each glass with a wedge or slice of clementine, if you like.

Nutritional information per portion: Energy 71kcal/299kJ; Protein 1.6g; Carbohydrate 16.4g, of which sugars 16g; Fat 0.4g, of which saturates 0.1g; Cholesterol 0mg; Calcium 56mg; Fibre 3.3g; Sodium 24mg.

Vitality juice

Fresh pears are a great energizer and can help give you a kick-start in the morning if you have a long, busy day ahead or a looming deadline to meet. This nutritious blend of ripe, juicy fruit, wheatgerm, yogurt, seeds and watercress makes a great-tasting tonic. If you would prefer a non-dairy version, use yogurt made from goat's milk, sheep's milk or soya.

MAKES 1 LARGE GLASS

25g/1oz watercress
1 large ripe pear
30ml/2 tbsp wheatgerm
150ml/¼ pint/⅔ cup natural (plain)
   yogurt
15ml/1 tbsp linseeds (flax seeds)
10ml/2 tsp lemon juice
mineral water (optional)
ice cubes

1 Roughly chop the watercress (you do not need to remove the tough stalks). Peel, core and roughly chop the pear.

2 Put the watercress and pear in a blender or food processor with the wheatgerm and blend until smooth. Scrape the mixture down from the side of the bowl if necessary.

3 Add the yogurt, seeds and lemon juice and blend until evenly combined. Thin with a little mineral water if the mixture is too thick and pour over ice cubes. Decorate with watercress.

Nutritional information per portion: Energy 346kcal/1454kJ; Protein 19.6g; Carbohydrate 39.9g, of which sugars 31.2g; Fat 13.4g, of which saturates 2.5g; Cholesterol 2mg; Calcium 461mg; Fibre 3.5g; Sodium 146mg.

Fennel fusion

Raw vegetables and apples combine to make a delicious juice. Fresh, cleansing fennel, with its distinctive aniseed flavour, blends well with both fruit and vegetables, while cabbage has natural anti-bacterial properties. You can also try celery in place of of fennel.

MAKES 1 GLASS

¹/₂ **small red cabbage**
¹/₂ **fennel bulb**
2 **apples**
15ml/1 tbsp **lemon juice**

1 This invigorating and cleansing drink is very easy to make. Roughly slice the cabbage and fennel and quarter the apples. Using a juice extractor, juice the vegetables and fruit.

2 Add the lemon juice to the juice mixture and stir. Pour into a glass and serve immediately.

Nutritional information per portion: Energy 183kcal/779kJ; Protein 5.5g; Carbohydrate 40.3g, of which sugars 39.9g; Fat 1.1g, of which saturates 0g; Cholesterol 0mg; Calcium 158mg; Fibre 2.8g; Sodium 42mg.

Apple and leaf lift-off

This delicious, rejuvenating blend of apple, grapes, fresh leaves and lime juice is great for treating skin, liver and kidney disorders. As apples feature in so many delicious, healthy blends, why not buy a large bag that will keep well in the refrigerator for several days.

MAKES 1 GLASS

1 **apple**
150g/5oz **white grapes**
small handful of fresh **coriander (cilantro)**, stalks included
25g/1oz **watercress** or **rocket (arugula)**
15ml/1 tbsp **lime juice**

1 Using a sharp knife, quarter the apple, removing the core if you like. Using a juice extractor, juice the apples and grapes, followed by the coriander and the watercress or rocket.

2 Add the lime juice to the fruit and herb mixture and stir well. Pour the mixture into a tall glass and serve immediately for maximum flavour.

Nutritional information per portion: Energy 135kcal/581kJ; Protein 3.8g; Carbohydrate 29.5g, of which sugars 29.5g; Fat 1.2g, of which saturates 0.3g; Cholesterol 0mg; Calcium 192mg; Fibre 3.6g; Sodium 53mg.

Gazpacho juice

Inspired by the classic Spanish soup, this fabulous juice looks and tastes delicious. Fresh salad vegetables can be thrown into a blender or food processor and whizzed up in moments to create a refreshing, invigorating drink. If you are planning to invite friends for a relaxing al fresco lunch, serve this cooling juice as an appetizer; it is perfect for a hot summer's day.

MAKES 4–5 GLASSES

½ **fresh red chilli**

800g/1¾lb **tomatoes, skinned**

½ **cucumber, roughly sliced**

1 **red (bell) pepper, seeded and cut into chunks**

1 **celery stick, chopped**

1 **spring onion (scallion), roughly chopped**

a small handful of fresh coriander (cilantro), stalks included, plus extra to decorate

juice of 1 lime

salt

ice cubes

1 Using a sharp knife, seed the chilli. Add to a blender or food processor with the tomatoes, cucumber, red pepper, celery, spring onion and coriander.

2 Blend well until smooth, scraping the vegetable mixture down from the side of the bowl, if necessary.

3 Add the lime juice and a little salt and blend. Pour into glasses. Add ice cubes and a few coriander leaves to serve.

Nutritional information per portion: Energy 32kcal/137kJ; Protein 1.5g; Carbohydrate 5.7g, of which sugars 5.6g; Fat 0.5g, of which saturates 0.2g; Cholesterol 0mg; Calcium 22mg; Fibre 1.9g; Sodium 19mg.

Ruby roots

Beetroot has the highest sugar content of any vegetable and, not surprisingly, makes one of the most delicious, sweet juices, with a vibrant red colour and a rich yet refreshing taste. Despite its firm texture, beetroot can be juiced raw and its intense flavour combines wonderfully with tangy citrus fruits and fresh root ginger. Enjoy this juice as a natural cleanser.

MAKES 1 LARGE GLASS

200g/7oz raw beetroot (beets)
1cm/¹/₂in piece fresh root ginger, peeled
1 large orange
ice cubes

1 Trim the beetroot and cut into quarters. Push half through a juicer, followed by the ginger and remaining beetroot.

2 Squeeze the juice from the orange and mix with the beetroot juice.

3 Pour the juice over ice cubes in a glass or clear glass cup. Serve immediately.

Nutritional information per portion: Energy 90kcal/385kJ; Protein 3.6g; Carbohydrate 19.6g, of which sugars 18.4g; Fat 0.3g, of which saturates 0g; Cholesterol 0mg; Calcium 45mg; Fibre 3.8g; Sodium 137mg.

Orange blossom

Avocados are extremely good for the skin, mainly because of their high vitamin E content. Combined with parsley, asparagus and orange, this juice makes a great cleanser and skin tonic. If you have a particular skin problem, drinking this juice regularly should really make a difference – it is very effective and much cheaper than many skin creams on the market.

MAKES 2 GLASSES

1 small avocado

small handful of parsley

75g/3oz tender asparagus spears

2 large oranges

squeeze of lemon juice

ice cubes

mineral water

orange wedges, to decorate

1 Halve the avocado and discard the stone (pit). Scoop the flesh into a blender or food processor. Remove any tough stalks from the parsley and add.

2 Roughly chop the asparagus and add to the avocado. Blend thoroughly until smooth, scraping the mixture down from the side of the bowl, if necessary.

3 Juice the oranges and add to the mixture with the lemon juice. Blend briefly until the mixture is very smooth. Pour the juice into two glasses until two-thirds full, then add ice cubes and mineral water. Decorate with chunky orange wedges.

COOK'S TIP

The orange and lemon juice in this blend means that the avocados will not discolour, so you might want to refrigerate a glass for later on. If it has thickened slightly, stir in a little extra mineral water.

Nutritional information per portion: Energy 123kcal/507kJ; Protein 2.3g; Carbohydrate 6.1g, of which sugars 5.4g; Fat 10g, of which saturates 2.1g; Cholesterol 0mg; Calcium 21mg; Fibre 2.4g; Sodium 9mg.

Bean good

Beansprouts are bursting with vitamins B and C, and are one of the few vegetables that actually increase in goodness after they are picked. Mixed with broccoli, another superfood, and naturally sweet fruits, this blend is a real tonic for your skin, hair and general health.

MAKES 1 LARGE OR 2 SMALL GLASSES

90g/3½oz broccoli
1 large pear
90g/3½oz/scant ½ cup beansprouts
200g/7oz green grapes
ice cubes and sliced green grapes

1 Using a small, sharp knife cut the broccoli into pieces small enough to fit through a juicer funnel.

2 Quarter the pear and carefully remove the core, then roughly chop the flesh into small chunks.

3 Push all the ingredients through the juicer. Pour into glasses and serve with ice cubes and sliced green grapes.

Nutritional information per portion: Energy 119kcal/505kJ; Protein 3.9g; Carbohydrate 25.5g, of which sugars 24.6g; Fat 0.8g, of which saturates 0.2g; Cholesterol 0mg; Calcium 56mg; Fibre 2.2g; Sodium 10mg.

Basil blush

Some herbs just don't juice well, losing their aromatic flavour and turning muddy and dull. Basil, however, is an excellent juicer, keeping its distinctive fresh fragrance. It makes the perfect partner for mild, refreshing cucumber and the ripest, juiciest tomatoes you can find.

MAKES 1–2 GLASSES

½ cucumber, peeled
a handful of fresh basil, plus extra to
    decorate
350g/12oz tomatoes
ice cubes

1 Quarter the cucumber lengthways – do not remove the seeds. Push it through a juicer with the basil, then do the same with the tomatoes.

2 Pour the blended tomato, basil and cucumber juice over cubes of ice in one or two glasses and serve decorated with a few fresh sprigs of basil.

COOK'S TIP
You don't have to peel the cucumber, but the juice will have a fresher, lighter colour without peel.

Nutritional information per portion: Energy 40kcal/168kJ; Protein 1.9g; Carbohydrate 7g, of which sugars 6.8g; Fat 0.7g, of which saturates 0.2g; Cholesterol 0mg; Calcium 31mg; Fibre 2.4g; Sodium 19mg.

Sugar snap

Sweet and juicy sugar snap peas are one of the most delicious vegetables to serve raw and they taste just as good when put through a juicer. The sweetness of the peas and the melon intensifies when they are juiced, while the fresh root ginger adds a definite edge.

MAKES 1 LARGE GLASS

1cm/$1/2$in piece fresh root ginger, peeled
$1/4$ honeydew or Galia melon
200g/7oz sugar snap peas, including pods
melon chunks and peas, to decorate

1 Using a sharp knife, chop the ginger. Scoop out the seeds from the melon and cut it into wedges. Cut away the skin, then chop the flesh into chunks.

2 Push the sugar snap peas through a juicer, followed by the chunks of melon and the slices of ginger. Serve chilled, with melon chunks and peas.

Nutritional information per portion: Energy 112kcal/476kJ; Protein 8.2g; Carbohydrate 19.6g, of which sugars 18g; Fat 0.6g, of which saturates 0g; Cholesterol 0mg; Calcium 114mg; Fibre 5.4g; Sodium 66mg.

Celery sensation

Savoury, almost salty, celery and sweet, green grapes make an astoundingly effective twosome when blended. A small handful of peppery watercress adds punch, but be careful not to add too much because its flavour intensifies greatly when the leaves are juiced.

MAKES 1 LARGE GLASS

2 celery sticks
a handful of watercress
200g/7oz/$13/4$ cups green grapes
1 leafy celery stick, to serve
crushed ice

1 Push the celery sticks through a juicer, followed by the watercress and the green grapes.

2 Put a leafy celery stick in a large glass to act as an edible swizzle stick and half-fill with crushed ice. Pour the juice over the ice and serve.

Nutritional information per portion: Energy 135kcal/579kJ; Protein 2.6g; Carbohydrate 31.5g, of which sugars 31.5g; Fat 0.8g, of which saturates 0.1g; Cholesterol 0mg; Calcium 136mg; Fibre 2.8g; Sodium 65mg.

Fresh and fruity

Ripe, juicy fruits make fabulous drinks,

whatever the combination of ingredients,

but, if you're looking for guidance, this

stunning assortment of recipes will set you

off in a frenzy of fruity blending. Whether

using blackcurrants, bananas or exotic

papayas, make sure you use the pick of

the crop so your juices are both highly

nutritious and tantalizingly tasty.

Apricot squash

The availability of fresh apricots can be rather erratic, so buy lots when you see them and make delicious apricot-based juices like this one. Choose sweet and juicy, ripe apricots, as they will act as a perfect foil to the tangy limes in this refreshing drink.

MAKES 2 GLASSES

2 limes

3 oranges

4 ripe apricots

several sprigs of lemon balm, plus extra
    to decorate

1 Squeeze the limes and oranges, either by hand or using a citrus juicer. Halve and stone the apricots.

2 Put the apricots in a blender or food processor with a little of the citrus juice and the lemon balm, and blend until smooth, scraping the mixture down from the side of the bowl, if necessary. Add the remaining juice and blend until completely smooth.

3 Pour into medium glasses and serve decorated with extra lemon balm.

Nutritional information per portion: Energy 46kcal/195kJ; Protein 0.9g; Carbohydrate 10.9g, of which sugars 10.9g; Fat 0.2g, of which saturates 0g; Cholesterol 0mg; Calcium 17mg; Fibre 1.1g; Sodium 9mg.

Sweet, sharp shock

The tingling combination of sweet red grape and tart apple is quite delicious. Grapes are full of natural sugars and, mixed with apple juice, they create a juice full of pep and zing. Grapes are also renowned for their cleansing properties, making this an ideal addition to any detox regime.

MAKES 2 SMALL GLASSES

150g/5oz/1¼ cups red grapes
1 red-skinned eating apple
1 small cooking apple
crushed ice

1 Slice some grapes and a sliver or two of apple for the decoration. Roughly chop the remaining apples. Push through a juicer with the grapes.

2 Pour over crushed ice. Decorate with the sliced fruit and serve immediately, in small wide glasses with lots of room for the fruit.

Nutritional information per portion: Energy 178kcal/763kJ; Protein 1.4g; Carbohydrate 45.4g, of which sugars 45.4g; Fat 0.4g, of which saturates 0g; Cholesterol 0mg; Calcium 30mg; Fibre 5g; Sodium 8mg.

Hum-zinger

This tropical cleanser contains 100 per cent fruit. It will help boost the digestive system and the kidneys, making your eyes sparkle, your hair shine and your skin glow. For the best results, use really ripe fruit, otherwise the juice may be sharp and flavourless.

MAKES 1 GLASS

¹/₂ **pineapple, peeled**
1 **small mango, peeled and pitted**
¹/₂ **small papaya, seeded and peeled**

1 Remove any "eyes" left in the pineapple, then cut all the fruit into rough chunks. Using a juice extractor, juice all of the fruit.

2 Alternatively, use a food processor or blender and process for 2–3 minutes until very smooth. Pour into a glass and serve immediately.

COOK'S TIP
Pineapple and mango can produce a very thick juice when blended so, if using this method, you might want to thin it down with a little mineral water before serving.

Nutritional information per portion: Energy 322kcal/1378kJ; Protein 3.7g; Carbohydrate 79.2g, of which sugars 78.7g; Fat 1.3g, of which saturates 0.1g; Cholesterol 0mg; Calcium 136mg; Fibre 13.1g; Sodium 21mg.

Citrus sparkle

This vibrantly coloured juice is full of zesty, natural citrus fruits packed with immune-boosting vitamin C, which can help to ward off winter colds and put a spring in your step. They are also renowned for their digestive cleansing properties.

MAKES 1 GLASS

1 **pink grapefruit**
1 **orange**
30ml/2 tbsp **lemon juice**

1 Using a sharp knife, cut the grapefruit and orange in half and squeeze out the juice using a citrus juicer.

2 Pour the mixed citrus juice into a tall glass, stir in the lemon juice and serve immediately.

Nutritional information per portion: Energy 92kcal/391kJ; Protein 2.6g; Carbohydrate 21.1g, of which sugars 21.1g; Fat 0.3g, of which saturates 0g; Cholesterol 0mg; Calcium 93mg; Fibre 4.1g; Sodium 11mg.

Pink and perky

This deliciously refreshing, rose-tinged blend of grapefruit and pear juice will keep you bright-eyed and bushy-tailed. It's perfect for a quick breakfast drink or as a pick-me-up later in the day when energy levels are flagging. If the grapefruit is particularly tart, serve with a little bowl of brown sugar to sweeten, or use brown sugar stirrers.

MAKES 2 TALL GLASSES

1 pink and 1 white grapefruit, halved
2 ripe pears
ice cubes

1 Take a thin slice from one grapefruit half and cut a few thin slices of pear. Roughly chop the remaining pear and push through a juicer.

2 Squeeze all the juice from the grapefruit halves. Mix the fruit juices together and serve over ice. Decorate with the grapefruit and pear slices.

Nutritional information per portion: Energy 108kcal/455kJ; Protein 1.8g; Carbohydrate 25.9g, of which sugars 25.9g; Fat 0.3g, of which saturates 0g; Cholesterol 0mg; Calcium 54mg; Fibre 5.4g; Sodium 10mg.

Red defender

Boost your body's natural defences with this delicious blend of red fruits. Watermelon and strawberries are a good source of vitamin C and the black watermelon seeds, like all other seeds, are rich in essential nutrients. However, if you really don't like the idea of blending the seeds, remove them first.

MAKES 2 GLASSES

200g/7oz/1³/₄ cups strawberries
small bunch red grapes, about 90g/3¹/₂oz
1 small wedge of watermelon

1 Hull the strawberries and halve them if they are large. Pull the grapes from their stalks. Cut away the skin from the watermelon.

2 Put the watermelon in a blender or food processor and blend until the seeds are broken up. Add the strawberries and grapes and blend until completely smooth, scraping the mixture down from the side of the bowl, if necessary. Serve in tall glasses.

Nutritional information per portion: Energy 85kcal/362kJ; Protein 1.5g; Carbohydrate 20.1g, of which sugars 20.1g; Fat 0.5g, of which saturates 0.1g; Cholesterol 0mg; Calcium 29mg; Fibre 1.5g; Sodium 9mg.

Apple shiner

Enjoy radiant skin and an instant energy boost with this cleansing fusion of apple, honeydew melon, red grapes and lemon. This is a good drink for spring, when all of these fruits are widely available. If you cannot get honeydew melon, use any other type as long as it's ripe.

MAKES 1 GLASS

$1/2$ **honeydew melon**
1 apple
90g/3$1/2$ oz red grapes
15ml/1 tbsp lemon juice

1 Using a sharp knife, cut the melon into quarters, scoop out the seeds with a spoon and slice the flesh away from the skin. Quarter the apple and remove the core if you like.

2 Using a juicer, juice the fruit. Alternatively, process the fruit in a food processor or blender for 2–3 minutes until smooth. Pour the juice into a glass, stir in the lemon juice and serve.

Nutritional information per portion: Energy 197kcal/842kJ; Protein 3.1g; Carbohydrate 47.8g, of which sugars 47.8g; Fat 0.7g, of which saturates 0g; Cholesterol 0mg; Calcium 79mg; Fibre 3.7g; Sodium 158mg.

Melon pick-me-up

This spicy blend of melon, pear and fresh root ginger will revive your body, stimulate your circulation and fire you into action. It is great at any time of day, whether you're enjoying a late breakfast or reviving yourself at the end of a day's work. Serve really chilled.

MAKES 1 GLASS

2 pears
$1/2$ **cantaloupe melon**
2.5cm/1in piece of fresh root ginger

1 Using a sharp knife, quarter the pears. Slice the melon in half and scoop out the seeds with a spoon. Cut the flesh away from the skin, then quarter.

2 Using a juicer, juice all the ingredients, pour into a tall glass and serve immediately.

Nutritional information per portion: Energy 240kcal/1017kJ; Protein 3.4g; Carbohydrate 58g, of which sugars 58g; Fat 0.8g, of which saturates 0g; Cholesterol 0mg; Calcium 98mg; Fibre 8.6g; Sodium 164mg.

Pomegranate plus

Sometimes difficult to find, pomegranates are worth buying when you see them for the chance to savour their exotic and distinctive flavour. A reddish skin is usually a sign that the seeds inside will be vibrant and sweet. Pomegranate juice makes a delicious base for this treat of a juice, which is mildly spiced with a hint of fresh ginger.

MAKES 2 GLASSES

2 pomegranates
4 fresh figs
15g/¹⁄₂oz fresh root ginger, peeled
10ml/2 tsp lime juice
ice cubes and lime wedges, to serve

1 Halve the pomegranates. Working over a bowl to catch the juices, pull away the skin to remove the jewel-like clusters of seeds.

2 Quarter the figs and roughly chop the ginger. Push the figs and ginger through a juicer. Push the pomegranate seeds through, reserving a few for decoration. Stir in the lime juice. Pour over ice cubes and lime wedges, then serve.

Nutritional information per portion: Energy 224kcal/951kJ; Protein 3.4g; Carbohydrate 52.3g, of which sugars 52.3g; Fat 1.6g, of which saturates 0g; Cholesterol 0mg; Calcium 233mg; Fibre 6.9g; Sodium 58mg.

Blue lagoon

Blueberries are not only an excellent source of betacarotene and vitamin C, they are also rich in flavonoids, which help to cleanse the system. Mixed with other dark red fruits, such as blackberries and grapes, they make a highly nutritious and irresistible blend that can be stored in the refrigerator and relished throughout the day.

MAKES 1 GLASS

90g/3¹/₂oz/scant 1 cup blackcurrants
   or blackberries
150g/5oz red grapes
130g/4¹/₂oz/generous 1 cup blueberries
ice cubes

1 Pull the blackcurrants, if using, and grapes from their stalks.

2 Push the fruits through a juicer, saving a few for decoration. Place the ice in a medium glass and pour over the juice. Decorate with the remaining fruit and serve.

COOK'S TIP
This is a really tangy wake-up drink that you might find a bit too sharp. Add a dash of sugar or honey, or top up with mineral water to dilute it slightly, if you like.

Nutritional information per portion: Energy 189kcal/805kJ; Protein 2.7g; Carbohydrate 47.2g, of which sugars 42g; Fat 0.1g, of which saturates 0g; Cholesterol 0mg; Calcium 74mg; Fibre 6.9g; Sodium 6mg.

Cherry berry trio

Strawberries and grapes have long been reputed to cleanse and purify the system, while cherries and strawberries are rich in vitamin C. This trio of plump, ripe fruits is packed with natural fruit sugars and needs absolutely no sweetening. To really spoil yourself (and undo all that cleansing power), try adding a splash of your favourite orange liqueur.

MAKES 2 LARGE GLASSES

200g/7oz/1³⁄₄ cups strawberries
250g/9oz/2¹⁄₄ cups red grapes
150g/5oz/1¹⁄₄ cups red cherries, pitted
ice cubes

1 Halve two or three strawberries and grapes and set aside with a few perfect cherries for decoration. Cut up any large strawberries, then push through a juicer with the remaining grapes and cherries.

2 Pour into glasses, top with the halved fruits, cherries and ice cubes, and serve immediately. To make a fun decoration, skewer a halved strawberry or grape on a cocktail stick (toothpick) and hang a cherry by its stem.

COOK'S TIP

Each year, the cherry season passes all too swiftly, so enjoy them in their full glory in this refreshing blend of sweet, fruity, fragrant red juices.

Nutritional information per portion: Energy 138kcal/587kJ; Protein 2g; Carbohydrate 33.9g, of which sugars 33.9g; Fat 0.3g, of which saturates 0g; Cholesterol 0mg; Calcium 42mg; Fibre 2.7g; Sodium 10mg.

Tropical calm

This delicious juice is packed with the cancer-fighting antioxidant betacarotene and can aid liver and kidney function to cleanse and purify the system. Enjoy this easy-to-make drink any time of day and top up with plenty of chilled sparkling water to quench a real thirst.

MAKES 1 GLASS

1 papaya
1/2 cantaloupe melon
90g/3 1/2 oz white grapes

1 Using a sharp knife, halve and skin the papaya, remove the seeds and then cut the flesh into rough slices. Halve the melon, scoop out the seeds and cut into quarters. Slice the flesh away from the skin and cut into chunks.

2 Juice the fruit using a juicer, or blend in a food processor or blender for a thicker juice. Serve immediately.

COOK'S TIP

Some varieties of papaya stay green when ripe, but most turn yellowy-orange and soften slightly. They bruise easily so don't buy any that have been knocked about. The seeds are edible but not particularly tasty, so they are usually discarded.

Nutritional information per portion: Energy 294kcal/1251kJ; Protein 4.4g; Carbohydrate 71.5g, of which sugars 71.5g; Fat 0.9g, of which saturates 0g; Cholesterol 0mg; Calcium 156mg; Fibre 11g; Sodium 146mg.

Strawberry soother

This comforting blend is made with fresh, ripe strawberries and a delicious peach or nectarine. Rich in vitamin C, calcium and healing phytochemicals, strawberries are a good addition to any detox diet, while peaches and nectarines are great for healthy skin.

MAKES 1 GLASS

1 peach or nectarine
225g/8oz/2 cups strawberries

1 Using a sharp knife, quarter the peach or nectarine and pull out the stone (pit). Cut the flesh into rough slices or chunks ready for juicing. Hull the strawberries.

2 Juice the fruit, using a juicer, or, if you prefer, blend in a food processor or blender for a thicker juice. Serve immediately.

Nutritional information per portion: Energy 84kcal/354kJ; Protein 2.5g; Carbohydrate 18.8g, of which sugars 18.8g; Fat 0.3g, of which saturates 0g; Cholesterol 0mg; Calcium 41mg; Fibre 3.5g; Sodium 14mg.

No gooseberry fool

Combine a sharp, tangy fruit like gooseberries with the sweetness of apples, greengages and kiwi fruit for a perfect blend of flavours – not too sweet, not too sharp, in fact just perfect. Even better, this drink is 100 per cent natural and is loaded with vital vitamins and minerals, meaning you can enjoy this delicious healthy tonic at any time of the day – guilt free.

MAKES 1 GLASS

1 kiwi fruit
2 greengages
1 eating apple
90g/3¹/₂oz/scant 1 cup gooseberries,
**   plus extra to decorate**
ice cubes

1 Peel the kiwi fruit, then halve and stone (pit) the greengages. Core and roughly chop the apple.

2 Push the kiwi fruit, greengages, apple and gooseberries through a juicer and pour over ice cubes into a glass. Add one or two gooseberries to decorate.

COOK'S TIP
Pink-tinged dessert gooseberries tend to be sweeter than the green ones, but both taste good in this refreshing drink. You might want to freeze a punnet of gooseberries so that you have a handy supply.

Nutritional information per portion: Energy 92kcal/391kJ; Protein 2.2g; Carbohydrate 20.3g, of which sugars 20.1g; Fat 0.8g, of which saturates 0g; Cholesterol 0mg; Calcium 51mg; Fibre 5.3g; Sodium 7mg.

Golden wonder

Ripe plums make delicious juices and work really well with the banana and passion fruit in this unconventional blend. Use yellow plums if you can find them, as they are irresistibly sweet and juicy, but red ones can easily be substituted as long as they're really soft and ripe. Vitamin rich and energizing, this drink is sure to set you up for the day.

MAKES 1 LARGE GLASS

2 passion fruit
2 yellow plums
1 small banana
about 15ml/1 tbsp lemon juice

1 Halve the passion fruit and, using a teaspoon, scoop the pulp into a blender or food processor. Using a small, sharp knife, halve and stone (pit) the plums and add to the blender or food processor.

2 Add the banana and lemon juice and blend the mixture until smooth, scraping the mixture down from the side of the bowl, if necessary. Then pour into a large glass and check the sweetness. Add a little more lemon juice, if you like.

Nutritional information per portion: Energy 108kcal/461kJ; Protein 2.1g; Carbohydrate 25.6g, of which sugars 23.7g; Fat 0.4g, of which saturates 0.1g; Cholesterol 0mg; Calcium 16mg; Fibre 2.8g; Sodium 8mg.

Minty melon cooler

The wonderfully juicy flesh of ripe melon seems somehow more fragrant and sweet when it is juiced. A dash of lime cuts through the sweetness perfectly and zips up the flavour, while refreshing, peppery mint makes a classic, cool companion to both. This mellow soother is equally calming and stimulating – what a combination.

MAKES 3–4 GLASSES

1 Galia or cantaloupe melon
several large mint sprigs
juice of 2 large limes
ice cubes
extra mint sprigs and lime slices, to decorate

1 Halve and seed the melon and cut into wedges. Cut one wedge into long, thin slices and reserve for decoration.

2 Cut the skin from the remaining melon wedges and push half the melon through a juicer. Strip the mint leaves from the sprigs, push them through the juicer, then juice the remaining melon.

3 Stir in the lime juice and then pour the juice over ice cubes in glasses. Decorate with mint sprigs and lime slices. Add a slice of melon to each glass and serve.

Nutritional information per portion: Energy 45kcal/191kJ; Protein 1g; Carbohydrate 10.5g, of which sugars 10.5g; Fat 0.2g, of which saturates 0g; Cholesterol 0mg; Calcium 25mg; Fibre 0.8g; Sodium 58mg.

Extra exotic coolers

Take juicing and blending into another league altogether with these enticing, adventurous and utterly irresistible creations. Try delicious sun-dried tomatoes with orange and tarragon or fabulous ripe pomegranates with Asian pears. Start experimenting and you'll soon discover that the possibilities are endless.

Passion fruit and orange crush

The scent and taste of this juice achieves that perfect balance of aromas and flavours. Sweet, zesty orange juice sits in perfect harmony with aromatic cardamom and intensely fragrant passion fruit to make the most heavenly juice imaginable. Along with the fabulous flavour and the glorious colour, you also get a generous shot of vitamin C.

MAKES 2 GLASSES

15ml/1 tbsp cardamom pods
15ml/1 tbsp caster (superfine) sugar
2 passion fruit
4 large oranges
ice cubes
halved orange slices, to decorate

1 Crush the cardamom pods with a mortar and pestle or place them in a small, metal bowl and pound with the end of a rolling pin. Simmer 90ml/6 tbsp water, the sugar, the pods, plus stray seeds, in a small pan for 5 minutes.

2 Halve the passion fruit and scoop the pulp into a small jug (pitcher). Squeeze the oranges and tip the juice into the jug. Strain the cardamom syrup through a fine sieve (strainer) into the fruit juice and whisk into a light froth.

3 Half-fill tall glasses with ice cubes and pour over the juice. Slip the orange slices into the glasses to serve as edible decoration.

Nutritional information per portion: Energy 128kcal/544kJ; Protein 3.2g; Carbohydrate 30g, of which sugars 30g; Fat 0.3g, of which saturates 0g; Cholesterol 0mg; Calcium 123mg; Fibre 4.8g; Sodium 16mg.

Lavender orange lush

This fragrant, lavender-scented juice is guaranteed to perk up a jaded palate in no time at all. Its heavenly aroma and distinct yet subtle taste are quite divine. Make plenty and keep it in the refrigerator, adding a few extra lavender sprigs to intensify the flavour, if you like. Additional sprigs of lavender make fun stirrers or a pretty garnish if serving at a party.

MAKES 4–6 GLASSES

10–12 lavender flowers, plus extra to serve
45ml/3 tbsp caster (superfine) sugar
8 large oranges
ice cubes

1 Pull the lavender flowers from their stalks and put them in a bowl with the sugar plus 120ml/4fl oz/$\frac{1}{2}$ cup boiling water. Stir until the sugar has dissolved, then leave to steep for 10 minutes.

2 Squeeze the oranges using a citrus juicer and pour the juice into a jug (pitcher). Strain the lavender syrup into the juice and chill.

3 Put a few ice cubes and a couple of lavender stirrers in some glasses, top up with the juice and serve.

Nutritional information per portion: Energy 91kcal/389kJ; Protein 1.9g; Carbohydrate 22g, of which sugars 22g; Fat 0.2g, of which saturates 0g; Cholesterol 0mg; Calcium 82mg; Fibre 2.8g; Sodium 9mg.

Apple infusion

East meets West in this fabulous fusion of fresh apple and fragrant spices. Ginger is combined with apple juice and exotic, fragrant lemon grass to make a deliciously refreshing cooler. As with many of these juices, it is well worth making double the quantity and keeping a supply in the refrigerator – as you will undoubtedly be back for more.

MAKES 2–3 GLASSES

1 lemon grass stalk	**ice cubes**
15g/¹⁄₂oz fresh root ginger, peeled	**sparkling water or real lemonade**
4 red-skinned eating apples	**red apple slices, to decorate**

1 Bruise the lemon grass stalk by pounding it with the tip of a rolling pin. Make several lengthways cuts through the stalk to open it up, keeping it intact at the thick end. Put the bruised stem into a small glass jug (pitcher).

2 Roughly chop the root ginger and cut the apples into chunks. Push the ginger and then the apples through a juicer.

3 Pour the juice into the jug and place in the refrigerator for at least 1 hour to let the flavours infuse.

4 Half-fill two or three tall glasses with ice cubes and red apple slices, if you like, and pour in the juice until it just covers the ice. Top up with sparkling water or lemonade, if you prefer, and serve immediately.

COOK'S TIP
Bruising the lemon grass stalk releases the subtle flavour, which pervades this cooler and provides a fragrant hint of the East.

Nutritional information per portion: Energy 47kcal/201kJ; Protein 0.4g; Carbohydrate 11.9g, of which sugars 11.9g; Fat 0.1g, of which saturates 0g; Cholesterol 0mg; Calcium 5mg; Fibre 2.1g; Sodium 3mg.

Watermelon and star anise fizz

The delicate taste of watermelon is surprisingly intense when juiced, so for balance, additional flavours need to be equally pronounced. A light syrup infused with liquorice-flavoured star anise is the perfect choice. For maximum impact, make sure the star anise is really fresh.

MAKES 2 TALL GLASSES

15g/¹/₂oz star anise
15ml/1 tbsp caster (superfine) sugar
500g/1¹/₄lb wedge of watermelon
sparkling mineral water

1 Roughly crush the star anise using a mortar and pestle.

2 Tip the crushed spice into a small pan and add the sugar and 90ml/6 tbsp water. Bring to the boil, stirring, then let it bubble for about 2 minutes. Remove from the heat and leave to steep for 10 minutes.

3 Cut off the watermelon rind. Cut the flesh into equal-sized chunks, removing all of the hard black seeds.

4 Push the melon chunks through a juicer. Strain the anise syrup through a fine sieve (strainer) and pour it into the melon juice. Stir thoroughly.

5 Fill two glasses two-thirds full with the juice, then top up with sparkling water and serve.

Nutritional information per portion: Energy 107kcal/459kJ; Protein 1.3g; Carbohydrate 25.6g, of which sugars 25.6g; Fat 0.8g, of which saturates 0.3g; Cholesterol 0mg; Calcium 22mg; Fibre 0.3g; Sodium 6mg.

Tarragon, orange and sun-dried tomato juice

Tomato juice fans will love this flavour-packed, vitalizing blend. Irresistible fresh orange adds extra vitamin C, while tarragon adds a lovely aromatic note. Add a dash of Tabasco or chilli sauce if you simply cannot resist the classic combination of chilli and tomato.

MAKES 2 GLASSES

4 large sprigs of tarragon, plus extra
   to garnish
500g/1lb 2oz tomatoes
2 large oranges
15ml/1 tbsp sun-dried tomato paste
ice cubes
ground black pepper

1 Pull the tarragon leaves from their stalks. Roughly chop the tomatoes. Push them through a juicer, alternating with the tarragon leaves.

2 Squeeze the juice from the oranges by hand or using a citrus juicer. Stir into the tomato and tarragon juice. Add the sun-dried tomato paste and stir well to mix all the ingredients together.

3 Place ice cubes into two glasses and pour over the juice. Serve immediately with pretty stirrers (if you have them), a sprinkling of black pepper to taste and tarragon sprigs to garnish.

Nutritional information per portion: Energy 93kcal/397kJ; Protein 3.5g; Carbohydrate 19g, of which sugars 19g; Fat 0.9g, of which saturates 0.3g; Cholesterol 0mg; Calcium 77mg; Fibre 4.8g; Sodium 47mg.

Honey and watermelon tonic

This refreshing juice will help to cool the body, calm the digestion and cleanse the system – and may even have aphrodisiac qualities. What more could you ask from a juice? The real magic of this drink, however, lies in its flavour. The light, watermelon taste is fresh on the palate, while the sticky, warm honey warms the throat – but it is the tart lime that gives it that edge.

MAKES 4 GLASSES

1 watermelon
1 litre/1³/₄ pints/4 cups chilled water
juice of 2 limes
clear honey
ice cubes, to serve

1 Using a sharp knife, chop the watermelon into chunks, cutting off the skin and discarding the black seeds.

2 Place the watermelon chunks in a large bowl, pour the chilled water over and leave to stand for 10 minutes.

3 Strain the watermelon chunks, then push them through a juicer.

4 Stir in the lime juice and sweeten to taste with honey. Pour into a jug (pitcher), add ice cubes and stir. Serve in wide, chunky glasses.

Nutritional information per portion: Energy 155kcal/665kJ; Protein 2.5g; Carbohydrate 35.5g, of which sugars 35.5g; Fat 1.5g, of which saturates 0.5g; Cholesterol 0mg; Calcium 35mg; Fibre 0.5g; Sodium 10mg.

Red hot chilli pepper

Sweet red peppers make a colourful, light juice that's best mixed with other ingredients for a full flavour impact. Courgettes add a subtle, almost unnoticeable body to the drink, while chilli and radishes add a wonderful kick of peppery heat. Freshly squeezed orange juice gives a delicious underlying zest to this extremely drinkable beverage.

MAKES 2–3 GLASSES

2 red (bell) peppers
1 fresh red chilli, seeded
150g/5oz courgettes (zucchini)
75g/3oz radishes
1 orange
ice cubes

1 Halve the red peppers, remove the cores and seeds, quarter the pieces and push them through a juicer with the chilli. Cut the courgettes into chunks, halve the radishes and push them through the juicer.

2 Squeeze the orange and stir the juice into the vegetable juice. Fill two or three glasses with ice, pour over the juice and serve immediately.

Nutritional information per portion: Energy 64kcal/269kJ; Protein 2.7g; Carbohydrate 12.2g, of which sugars 11.8g; Fat 0.8g, of which saturates 0.2g; Cholesterol 0mg; Calcium 45mg; Fibre 3.2g; Sodium 10mg.

Kiwi and stem ginger spritzer

The delicate, refreshingly tangy flavour of kiwi fruit becomes sweeter and more intense when the flesh is juiced. Choose plump, unwrinkled fruits that give a little when gently pressed as under-ripe fruits will produce a slightly bitter taste. A single kiwi fruit contains more than one day's vitamin C requirement, so this juice will really boost the system.

MAKES 1 TALL GLASS

2 kiwi fruit
1 piece preserved stem ginger, plus 15ml/
**   1 tbsp syrup from the ginger jar**
sparkling mineral water

1 Using a sharp knife, roughly chop the kiwi fruit and the ginger. (For a better colour you can peel the kiwi fruit first, but this is not essential.)

2 Push the ginger and kiwi fruit through a juicer and pour the juice into a jug (pitcher). Stir in the ginger syrup.

3 Pour the juice into a tall glass, then top up with sparkling mineral water and serve immediately.

COOK'S TIP
Kiwis are a subtropical fruit, not a tropical one, so it is best to store them in the refrigerator before using. If you want them to ripen quickly, store in a closed plastic bag with an apple, pear or banana.

Nutritional information per portion: Energy 104kcal/439kJ; Protein 1.4g; Carbohydrate 24.6g, of which sugars 24.2g; Fat 0.6g, of which saturates 0g; Cholesterol 0mg; Calcium 32mg; Fibre 2.3g; Sodium 45mg.

Fragrant fruits

This blend of sweet and subtle fruits packs a surprising punch. It combines a splash of lemon and a hint of fresh root ginger to add zest and bite without overpowering the delicate, fragrant flavours of lychee, cantaloupe and pear. Other types of melon can be used in place of the cantaloupe, but you will lose the pretty colour that is part of this juice's appeal.

MAKES 2 TALL GLASSES

10 lychees

1 large pear

300g/11oz wedge cantaloupe melon, rind removed

2cm/³/₄in piece fresh root ginger, roughly chopped

squeeze of lemon juice

crushed ice

mint sprigs, to decorate

1 Peel and stone (pit) the lychees and, using a sharp knife, cut both the pear and the melon into large chunks.

2 Push the ginger through a juicer, followed by the lychees, pear and melon. Sharpen the flavour with a little of the lemon juice to taste.

3 Place the crushed ice and one or two mint sprigs in tall glasses and pour over the juice. Place some more mints sprigs on top to decorate, then serve the juice immediately – before the ice melts.

Nutritional information per portion: Energy 110kcal/466kJ; Protein 1.7g; Carbohydrate 26.7g, of which sugars 26.7g; Fat 0.3g, of which saturates 0g; Cholesterol 0mg; Calcium 33mg; Fibre 2.8g; Sodium 50mg.

Pink gin

Juniper berries are a vital ingredient in the making of gin and, not surprisingly, they exude distinct gin-like aromas in this fabulous drink. For a good colour, this is best made using early, forced rhubarb, which gives the juice a characteristic pink blush. Top up the gin with chilled sparkling water, or use real lemonade for a delicious, tangy taste.

MAKES 4 GLASSES

600g/1lb 6oz rhubarb
finely grated rind and juice of 2 limes
75g/3oz/6 tbsp caster (superfine) sugar
15ml/1 tbsp juniper berries, lightly
    crushed
ice cubes
lime slices, quartered
sparkling mineral water, soda water (club
    soda) or real lemonade

1 Using a sharp knife, chop the rhubarb into 2cm/³⁄₄in lengths and place in a pan with the lime rind and juice.

2 Add the sugar, crushed juniper berries and 90ml/6 tbsp water. Cover with a tightly fitting lid and cook for 6–8 minutes until the rhubarb is just tender. (Test by prodding the rhubarb with the tip of a knife.)

3 Transfer the rhubarb to a food processor or blender and process to form a smooth purée. Press the mixture through a coarse sieve (strainer) into a bowl and set the strained juice aside until completely cooled.

4 Half-fill medium glasses with the juice. Add ice cubes and lime slices and top up with sparkling mineral water, soda water or lemonade, and serve.

Nutritional information per portion: Energy 85kcal/363kJ; Protein 1.5g; Carbohydrate 20.8g, of which sugars 20.8g; Fat 0.2g, of which saturates 0g; Cholesterol 0mg; Calcium 150mg; Fibre 2.1g; Sodium 6mg.

Spiced pomegranate and Asian pear fizz

Sweet but with a milder flavour than traditional pears, Asian pears make a good partner for the fresh tang of pomegranates. Juice the fruits in advance if you have the time, so the spice can mellow into the fruits, all ready for topping up with fizzy tonic water.

MAKES 2 GLASSES

2 Asian pears
1.5ml/¼ tsp ground allspice
1 pomegranate
5–10ml/1–2 tsp clear honey
ice cubes
tonic water
pear wedges and pomegranate seeds, to decorate

1 Using a small, sharp knife, chop the pears into large chunks. Mix the allspice in a jug (pitcher) with 15ml/1 tbsp boiling water.

2 Halve the pomegranate. Working over the jug to catch the juices, peel away the skin and layers of pith to leave the clusters of seeds.

3 Push the pears and pomegranate seeds through a juicer and mix together in the jug with the allspice. Stir in a little honey to sweeten, then chill.

4 Pour the juice into glasses until two-thirds full. Serve with ice cubes, pear wedges and pomegranate seeds to decorate. Top up with tonic water.

Nutritional information per portion: Energy 92kcal/391kJ; Protein 0.6g; Carbohydrate 23.3g, of which sugars 23.3g; Fat 0.2g, of which saturates 0g; Cholesterol 0mg; Calcium 19mg; Fibre 4.1g; Sodium 6mg.

Elderflower, plum and ginger juice

Captured in cordials and juices, the aromatic flavour of elderflowers can be enjoyed all year round. Here it is used with fresh root ginger to give an exotic boost to sweet, juicy plums. Serve this juice just as it is over plenty of crushed ice or top up with sparkling water.

MAKES 2–3 GLASSES

15g/½oz fresh root ginger
500g/1lb 2oz ripe plums
125ml/4½fl oz/generous ½ cup sweetened elderflower cordial
ice cubes
sparkling water or tonic water
mint sprigs and plum slices, to decorate

1 Roughly chop the ginger without peeling. Halve and stone (pit) the plums.

2 Push half the plums through a juicer, followed by the ginger, then the remaining plums. Mix the juice with the elderflower cordial in a jug (pitcher).

3 Place the ice cubes into two large or three medium-sized glasses. Pour over the juice until the glasses are two-thirds full. Place the mint sprigs and plum slices on top to decorate and top up with sparkling mineral water or tonic water. Serve immediately.

COOK'S TIP
The elder is a tree or bush with perfumed, yellowish-white flowers and tiny black-violet berries, both of which are thought to be medicinal.

Nutritional information per portion: Energy 105kcal/450kJ; Protein 1g; Carbohydrate 26.6g, of which sugars 26.6g; Fat 0.2g, of which saturates 0g; Cholesterol 0mg; Calcium 25mg; Fibre 2.7g; Sodium 7mg.

Thyme-scented plum lush

Make this divine drink in the early autumn when plums are at their sweetest and best. Their silky smooth flesh blends down to produce the most wonderfully textured smoothie, while delicately scented lemon thyme and honey complement the flavour perfectly. This luxurious juice is easy to make and has an irresistible fragrance that is at once warming and refreshing.

MAKES 2–3 GLASSES

400g/14oz red plums
30–45ml/2–3 tbsp clear honey
15ml/1 tbsp chopped fresh lemon thyme,
  plus extra thyme sprigs to decorate
100g/3¾oz crushed ice

1 Using a sharp knife, halve and stone (pit) the plums and put in a blender or food processor. Add 30ml/2 tbsp of the honey and the lemon thyme and blend until smooth, scraping down the side of the bowl, if necessary.

2 Add the ice and blend until slushy. Taste for sweetness, adding a little more honey if necessary. Pour into glasses and serve immediately, decorated with a sprig of thyme.

Nutritional information per portion: Energy 77kcal/330kJ; Protein 0.8g; Carbohydrate 19.4g, of which sugars 19.4g; Fat 0.1g, of which saturates 0g; Cholesterol 0mg; Calcium 18mg; Fibre 2.1g; Sodium 4mg.

Iced pear aniseed

Aniseed is a spice widely used in cooking, not only in sweet and savoury dishes but as the dominant flavour in many alcoholic drinks like pastis, ouzo and raki. If these flavours appeal to you – without the alcohol, though – you'll love this deliciously spicy pear-based infusion. Serve in small glasses over plenty of crushed ice. Add a slice or two of fresh pear, if you like.

MAKES 2–3 GLASSES

30ml/2 tbsp aniseeds
30ml/2 tbsp caster (superfine) sugar
3 soft, ripe pears
10ml/2 tsp lemon juice
crushed ice

1 Using a mortar and pestle, lightly crush the aniseeds. (Alternatively, use a small bowl and the end of a rolling pin to crush the seeds.) Put in a small pan with the sugar and 100ml/3$^{1}/_{2}$fl oz/ scant $^{1}/_{2}$ cup water. Heat very gently, stirring until the sugar has dissolved. Bring to the boil and boil for 1 minute. Pour the syrup into a small jug (pitcher) and leave to cool completely.

2 Quarter the pears and remove the cores. Push through a juicer. Add the lemon juice. Strain the syrup into the pear juice and chill until ready to serve. Pour over crushed ice in small glasses.

Nutritional information per portion: Energy 99kcal/422kJ; Protein 0.5g; Carbohydrate 25.4g, of which sugars 25.4g; Fat 0.2g, of which saturates 0g; Cholesterol 0mg; Calcium 22mg; Fibre 3.3g; Sodium 5mg.

Easy breakfast blends

Breakfast is the most important meal of the day but also the most neglected, so give yourself a kick-start with these fuel-packed, imaginative drinks. Made in minutes and easier to digest than a bowl of cereal, fabulous fresh fruit juices and decadent mocha smoothies provide the perfect early-morning boost.

Citrus tingler

With a reliable abundance of oranges available throughout the year, it is all too easy to overlook the more unusual citrus fruits. This citrus trio combines the sharp, grapefruit-like fragrance of pomelos, the mild sweetness of Ugli fruit and the vibrant colour of flavour-packed mandarins.

MAKES 1 GLASS

1 pomelo
1 Ugli fruit
1 mandarin
squeeze of lemon or lime juice (optional)
ice cubes
citrus fruit slices, to decorate

1 Halve the fruits and squeeze the juice using a citrus juicer. Add a little squeeze of lemon or lime juice, if you like, to create a sharper flavour.

2 Pour the juice into a tall glass and add ice cubes and a few citrus fruit slices to decorate. Serve immediately.

COOK'S TIP
This easy-to-make refresher can quickly prove popular first thing in the morning. If you are making breakfast for your partner or the family, simply multiply the ingredients by the number of people that you are serving – or even better, let them make their own.

Nutritional information per portion: Energy 111kcal/466kJ; Protein 2.9g; Carbohydrate 25.2g, of which sugars 25.2g; Fat 0.4g, of which saturates 0g; Cholesterol 0mg; Calcium 86mg; Fibre 4.6g; Sodium 11mg.

Raspberry and oatmeal smoothie

Just a spoonful or so of oatmeal gives substance to this tangy, invigorating drink. If you can, prepare it ahead of time because soaking the raw oats helps to break down the starch into natural sugars that are easy to digest. The smoothie will thicken up in the refrigerator so you might need to stir in a little extra juice or mineral water just before serving.

MAKES 1 LARGE GLASS

25ml/1¹/₂ tbsp medium oatmeal
150g/5oz/scant 1 cup raspberries
5–10ml/1–2 tsp clear honey
45ml/3 tbsp natural (plain) yogurt

1 Spoon the oatmeal into a heatproof bowl. Pour in 120ml/4fl oz/¹/₂ cup boiling water and leave to stand for about 10 minutes.

2 Put the soaked oats in a blender or food processor and add all but two or three of the raspberries, the honey and about 30ml/2 tbsp of the yogurt. Process until smooth, scraping down the side of the bowl if necessary.

3 Pour the raspberry and oatmeal smoothie into a large glass, swirl in the remaining yogurt and top with the reserved raspberries.

Nutritional information per portion: Energy 171kcal/728kJ; Protein 7.2g; Carbohydrate 31.1g, of which sugars 12.9g; Fat 3g, of which saturates 0.3g; Cholesterol 1mg; Calcium 131mg; Fibre 4.8g; Sodium 50mg.

Sweet dream

A soothing blend guaranteed to wake you up slowly, this fruity threesome is naturally sweet so there is no need for any additional sugar. Fresh grapefruit juice marries brilliantly with the dried fruits, and rich creamy yogurt makes a delicious contrast of colour and flavour – simply perfect to sip over a leisurely breakfast while reading the newspaper.

MAKES 2 GLASSES

25g/1oz/scant ¼ cup dried figs or dates, stoned (pitted)

50g/2oz/¼ cup ready-to-eat prunes

25g/1oz/scant ¼ cup sultanas (golden raisins)

1 grapefruit

350ml/12fl oz/1½ cups full cream (whole) milk

30ml/2 tbsp Greek (US strained plain) yogurt

1 Put the dried fruits in a blender or food processor. Squeeze the grapefruit juice and add to the machine. Blend until smooth, scraping the mixture down from the side of the bowl, if necessary. Add the milk and blend until completely smooth.

2 Using a teaspoon, tap a spoonful of the yogurt around the inside of each of two tall glasses. Pour in the fruit mixture and serve immediately.

Nutritional information per portion: Energy 246kcal/1033kJ; Protein 8.6g; Carbohydrate 38.3g, of which sugars 38.3g; Fat 7.4g, of which saturates 4.5g; Cholesterol 25mg; Calcium 301mg; Fibre 3.7g; Sodium 103mg.

Creamy banana boost

Bananas are a great energy food. They are packed with valuable nutrients and healthy carbohydrates, and they also fill you up. Blended with pineapple, dates, lemon juice and creamy milk, this delicious concoction will keep you going for hours.

MAKES 2–3 TALL GLASSES

¹/₂ pineapple
4 Medjool dates, stoned (pitted)
1 small ripe banana
juice of 1 lemon
300ml/¹/₂ pint/1¹/₄ cups very cold full cream (whole) milk or
   soya milk

1 Using a small, sharp knife, cut away the skin and core from the pineapple. Roughly chop the flesh and put it in a blender or food processor, then add the pitted dates.

2 Peel and chop the banana and add it to the rest of the fruit together with the lemon juice.

3 Blend thoroughly until smooth, stopping to scrape the mixture down from the side of the bowl with a rubber spatula, if necessary.

4 Add the milk to the blender or food processor and process briefly until well combined. Pour the smoothie into tall glasses and serve immediately.

Nutritional information per portion: Energy 187kcal/793kJ; Protein 4.7g; Carbohydrate 34.6g, of which sugars 34g; Fat 4.3g, of which saturates 2.5g; Cholesterol 14mg; Calcium 152mg; Fibre 2.5g; Sodium 48mg.

Zesty soya smoothie

Whizzed up with freshly squeezed orange juice, tangy lemon and a little fragrant honey, tofu is transformed into a smooth, creamy, nutritious and delicious treat. Most people would not think to add tofu to a blended drink, but try it – you will be genuinely surprised.

MAKES 1 LARGE GLASS

2 oranges
15ml/1 tbsp lemon juice
20–25ml/4–5 tsp sunflower honey or herb honey
150g/5oz tofu
long, thin strips of pared orange rind, to decorate

1 Finely grate the rind of one orange and set aside. Use a citrus juicer to juice both oranges and pour the juice into a food processor or blender. Add the grated orange rind, lemon juice, sunflower or herb honey and tofu.

2 Whizz the ingredients until smooth and creamy, then pour into a glass. Decorate with the pared orange rind and serve.

COOK'S TIP

If you prefer a smooth drink, strain the liquid through a sieve (strainer) after blending to remove the orange rind.

Nutritional information per portion: Energy 350kcal/1483kJ; Protein 15.6g; Carbohydrate 60.9g, of which sugars 60.3g; Fat 6.6g, of which saturates 0.8g; Cholesterol 0mg; Calcium 908mg; Fibre 5.1g; Sodium 26mg.

Muesli smoothly

Another great breakfast booster, this store-cupboard smoothie can be a lifesaver if you've run out of fresh fruit. It's also a perfect option for breakfast in bed without the crumbs. Any extra drink can be covered and stored overnight in the refrigerator, although you'll probably need to add more milk in the morning as it will undoubtedly thicken on standing.

MAKES 2 GLASSES

1 piece preserved stem ginger, plus 30ml/2 tbsp syrup from the ginger jar
50g/2oz/¼ cup ready-to-eat dried apricots, halved or quartered
40g/1½oz/scant ½ cup natural muesli (granola)
about 200ml/7fl oz/scant 1 cup semi-skimmed (low-fat) milk

1 Chop the preserved ginger and put it in a blender or food processor with the syrup, apricots, muesli and milk.

2 Process until smooth, adding more milk if necessary. Serve in wide glasses.

COOK'S TIP

Apricot and ginger are perfect partners in this divine drink. It makes an incredibly healthy, tasty breakfast, but is so delicious and indulgent that you could even serve it as a dessert after a summer meal.

Nutritional information per portion: Energy 203kcal/862kJ; Protein 6.4g; Carbohydrate 40.1g, of which sugars 30.9g; Fat 3.2g, of which saturates 1.3g; Cholesterol 6mg; Calcium 163mg; Fibre 2.9g; Sodium 163mg.

Orange and raspberry smoothie

This exquisite blend combines the sharp-sweet taste of raspberries and the refreshing fruitiness of oranges with smooth yogurt. It tastes like creamy, fruit heaven in a glass. Even better, it takes just minutes to prepare, making it perfect as a quick breakfast juice for people in a hurry or, indeed, as a refreshing drink at any other time of day.

MAKES 2–3 GLASSES

250g/9oz/1^1/$_3$ cups raspberries, chilled
200ml/7fl oz/scant 1 cup natural (plain) yogurt, chilled
300ml/^{1}/$_2$ pint/1^1/$_4$ cups freshly squeezed orange juice, chilled

1 Place the raspberries and yogurt in a blender or food processor and process for about 1 minute until the mixture is smooth and creamy.

2 Add the orange juice to the raspberry and yogurt mixture and process for another 30 seconds or until thoroughly combined. Pour into tall glasses and serve immediately.

COOK'S TIP
For a super-chilled version, use frozen raspberries instead of fresh. You may, though, need to blend the raspberries and yogurt for a little longer to get a really smooth result.

Nutritional information per portion: Energy 94kcal/401kJ; Protein 5.1g; Carbohydrate 17.6g, of which sugars 17.6g; Fat 1g, of which saturates 0.4g; Cholesterol 1mg; Calcium 158mg; Fibre 2.2g; Sodium 68mg.

Peachy pleasure

When juiced together, apricots, peaches and kumquats produce the most amazingly vibrant, flavoursome orange-coloured juice with a big kick. The natural sugar content of apricots and peaches varies greatly, so add some honey to get the taste just right.

MAKES 2 GLASSES

4 kumquats
6 ripe apricots, stoned (pitted)
2 peaches, stoned (pitted)
clear honey, to taste
ice cubes

1 Using a small, sharp knife, roughly chop the kumquats and cut the apricots and peaches into large chunks. (There is no need to peel the fruit.)

2 Push the kumquat pieces through a juicer, followed by the apricot and peach chunks, alternating the fruit as you go to ensure they mix well.

3 Fill two large glasses with ice cubes and pour the fruit juice over the ice.

4 Stir in a little honey to the juice and taste. Add just a little more honey if the juice is not sweet enough. (However, be careful not to add too much honey, or it will overpower the other flavours and spoil the drink.) Serve immediately.

Nutritional information per portion: Energy 78kcal/335kJ; Protein 2.3g; Carbohydrate 18g, of which sugars 18g; Fat 0.3g, of which saturates 0g; Cholesterol 0mg; Calcium 31mg; Fibre 3.8g; Sodium 4mg.

Tropicana

Even in winter this delicious tropical drink can brighten your day. Any blend of tropical fruits makes a fabulous juice as long as they are ripe. When underripe, persimmon and guavas can both be bitter if juiced, so leave them to ripen for a few days before using.

MAKES 2–3 GLASSES

1 large papaya
1 persimmon
1 large guava
juice of 2 oranges
2 passion fruit, halved

1 Halve the papaya, then scoop out and discard the black seeds. Using a small, sharp knife, cut the papaya, persimmon and guava flesh into large chunks of roughly the same size. (There's no need to peel them.)

2 Push the papaya through a juicer, followed by the persimmon and the guava. Pour the juice into a jug (pitcher), then add the orange juice and scoop in the passion fruit pulp. Whisk and chill until ready to serve.

COOK'S TIP
When chopping the fruit, cut some into chunky slices and reserve for decoration, if you like. Otherwise, throw in some fruit chunks at the end to add some texture.

Nutritional information per portion: Energy 85kcal/361kJ; Protein 1.8g; Carbohydrate 19.3g, of which sugars 19.2g; Fat 0.6g, of which saturates 0g; Cholesterol 0mg; Calcium 45mg; Fibre 6g; Sodium 17mg.

Mango and lime lassi

Inspired by the classic Indian drink, this tangy, fruity blend is great for breakfast or as a delicious pick-me-up at any time of day. Soft, ripe mango blended with yogurt and sharp, zesty lime and lemon juice makes a wonderfully thick, cooling drink that's packed with energy. It can also be enjoyed as a mellow soother when you need to unwind.

MAKES 2 TALL GLASSES

1 mango
finely grated rind and juice of 1 lime
15ml/1 tbsp lemon juice
5–10ml/1–2 tsp caster (superfine) sugar
100ml/3½fl oz/scant ½ cup natural
   (plain) yogurt
mineral water
1 extra lime, halved, to serve

1 Peel the mango and cut the flesh from the stone (pit). Put the flesh into a blender or food processor and add the lime rind and juice.

2 Add the lemon juice, sugar and natural yogurt. Whizz until completely smooth, scraping down the sides of the bowl, if necessary. Stir in a little mineral water to thin it down.

3 Serve immediately, with half a lime on the side of each glass so that more juice can be squeezed in, if desired.

Nutritional information per portion: Energy 81kcal/344kJ; Protein 3.1g; Carbohydrate 17g, of which sugars 16.7g; Fat 0.7g, of which saturates 0.4g; Cholesterol 1mg; Calcium 106mg; Fibre 2g; Sodium 43mg.

Big breakfast

Easy to prepare and even easier to drink, this energy-packed smoothie makes a great start to the day. Bananas and sesame seeds provide the perfect fuel in the form of slow-release carbohydrate that will keep you going all morning, while fresh and zesty orange juice and sweet, scented mango will set your tastebuds tingling first thing.

MAKES 2 GLASSES

½ **mango**

1 **banana**

1 **large orange**

30ml/2 tbsp **wheat bran**

15ml/1 tbsp **sesame seeds**

10–15ml/2–3 tsp **honey**

1 Using a small, sharp knife, skin the mango, then slice the flesh off the stone (pit). Peel the banana and break it into short lengths, then place it in a blender or food processor with the mango.

2 Squeeze the juice from the orange and add to the blender or food processor along with the bran, sesame seeds and honey. Whizz until the mixture is smooth and creamy, then pour into glasses and serve.

Nutritional information per portion: Energy 123kcal/523kJ; Protein 3.4g; Carbohydrate 26.9g, of which sugars 23.7g; Fat 1g, of which saturates 0.2g; Cholesterol 0mg; Calcium 40mg; Fibre 3.6g; Sodium 5mg.

Dairy-free deluxe

Prunes, apples, oranges and soya milk may seem like an unusual combination but the results are absolutely fabulous. Sweet, caramel-rich and very drinkable, this is a great milkshake for both adults and children, and, of course, for anyone on a dairy-free diet.

MAKES 1 GLASS

2 small eating apples
5 ready-to-eat pitted prunes
juice of 1 orange
60ml/4 tbsp soya milk
ice cubes

1 Using a small, sharp knife, remove the core from the apples and chop into chunks – but do not peel them. Push half the chopped apple through a juicer, followed by the prunes and the remaining chopped apple.

2 Pour the apple and prune juice into a jug (pitcher) and add the orange juice and soya milk. Whisk lightly until smooth and frothy. Pour into a chunky glass and serve immediately, adding a few cubes of ice.

COOK'S TIP

Any eating apples can be used for this drink. If you prefer a tart flavour, opt for a Granny Smith or a Cox's Pippin; if not, go for a sweet apple like the Royal Gala.

Nutritional information per portion: Energy 248kcal/1059kJ; Protein 5.1g; Carbohydrate 56.7g, of which sugars 56.7g; Fat 1.6g, of which saturates 0.2g; Cholesterol 0mg; Calcium 55mg; Fibre 9g; Sodium 39mg.

Pear flair

For a truly refreshing combination, you can't do much better than a mixture of juicy pears and grapes. Wheatgerm adds body for a sustained energy fix and soya yogurt turns the juice into a protein-packed milkshake with a lusciously light and frothy topping.

MAKES 1 LARGE GLASS

1 large pear
150g/5oz/1¼ cups green grapes
15ml/1 tbsp wheatgerm
60ml/4 tbsp soya yogurt
ice cubes

1 Using a vegetable peeler, peel the pear and chop the flesh into large chunks of roughly the same size.

2 Push half the pear chunks through a juicer, followed by the grapes and then the remaining chunks of pear. Transfer the juice to a small jug (pitcher).

3 Add the wheatgerm to the yogurt and then stir to mix thoroughly.

4 Pour into the pear and grape juice, whisking until light and frothy. Pour the milkshake over ice cubes and serve.

COOK'S TIP

If you would prefer to use a dairy yogurt rather than the soya variety, substitute with the type of your choice. It is better that you stick with a natural (plain) yogurt as plenty of fruity flavour is gained from the pear and the grapes. Look out for the 0 per cent fat varieties.

Nutritional information per portion: Energy 247kcal/1048kJ; Protein 8.1g; Carbohydrate 47.1g, of which sugars 42.8g; Fat 2.8g, of which saturates 0.6g; Cholesterol 1mg; Calcium 44mg; Fibre 6.7g; Sodium 8mg.

Late breakfast

This energizing blend is simply bursting with goodness, just what you need when the morning has got off to a slow start. Not only is tofu a perfect source of protein, it is also rich in minerals and contains nutrients that protect against dangerous diseases. Blended with seeds and vitamin-rich strawberries, this creamy blend should see you through until lunchtime. Store any leftovers in the refrigerator for later in the day or the following morning.

MAKES 2 GLASSES

250g/9oz firm tofu

200g/7oz/1³/₄ cups strawberries

45ml/3 tbsp pumpkin or sunflower seeds, plus extra for sprinkling

30–45ml/2–3 tbsp clear honey

juice of 2 large oranges

juice of 1 lemon

1 Roughly chop the tofu, then hull and roughly chop the strawberries. Reserve a few strawberry chunks.

2 Put all the ingredients in a blender or food processor and blend until completely smooth, scraping the mixture down from the side of the bowl, if necessary.

3 Pour into tumblers and sprinkle with extra seeds and strawberry chunks.

Nutritional information per portion: Energy 310kcal/1296kJ; Protein 15.7g; Carbohydrate 26.9g, of which sugars 22.6g; Fat 16.1g, of which saturates 1.7g; Cholesterol 0mg; Calcium 684mg; Fibre 2.5g; Sodium 19mg.

A good fix

While some people thrive on a glass of freshly juiced fruits first thing in the morning, others can't quite get going without their daily caffeine fix in the form of strong coffee. This gorgeous mocha smoothie combines decadent dark chocolate and caffeine-rich coffee in a deliciously frothy energizing mix. This is an intensely sweet and indulgent way to start the day – so it's best not to treat yourself too often.

MAKES 1 LARGE GLASS

40g/1½ oz plain (semisweet) chocolate, plus extra for decoration

5–10ml/1–2 tsp instant espresso powder

300ml/½ pint/1¼ cups full cream (whole) milk

30ml/2 tbsp double (heavy) cream (optional)

ice cubes

cocoa powder (unsweetened), for dusting

1 Chop the chocolate into pieces and place in a small, heavy pan with the espresso powder and 100ml/3½fl oz/ scant ½ cup of the milk. Heat very gently, stirring with a wooden spoon, until the chocolate has melted. Remove from the heat and pour into a bowl. Leave to cool for 10 minutes.

2 Add the remaining milk and cream, if using, and whisk the mixture together until smooth and frothy – you could use a handheld blender wand. Pour the smoothie over ice cubes in a large glass or mug and serve sprinkled with cocoa powder and chocolate shavings.

Nutritional information per portion: Energy 402kcal/1677kJ; Protein 11.9g; Carbohydrate 38.9g, of which sugars 38.5g; Fat 22.9g, of which saturates 14.2g; Cholesterol 44mg; Calcium 367mg; Fibre 1g; Sodium 131mg.

Cool, smooth and creamy

Milkshakes can be either refreshing and fruity or smooth and creamy, but they are always a treat. Inspiring ingredients include brownies and fruit tea, and there are several shakes made with more traditional flavours such as vanilla or banana. Fun for kids and nostalgically appealing for adults, comfort drinks never looked or tasted so good.

Simply strawberry

Nothing evokes a sense of summer wellbeing more than the scent and flavour of sweet, juicy strawberries. This recipe uses an abundance of these fragrant fruits so, if possible, make it when the season is right and local ones are at their most plentiful.

MAKES 2 GLASSES

400g/14oz/3¹/₂ cups strawberries, plus extra to decorate

30–45ml/2–3 tbsp icing (confectioners') sugar

200g/7oz/scant 1 cup Greek (US strained plain) yogurt

60ml/4 tbsp single (light) cream

1 Hull the strawberries and place them in a blender or food processor with 30ml/2 tbsp of the icing sugar. Blend to a smooth purée, scraping the mixture down from the side of the bowl with a rubber spatula, if necessary.

2 Add the yogurt and cream and blend again until smooth and frothy. Check the sweetness, adding just a little more sugar if you find the flavour too sharp. Pour into glasses and serve decorated with extra strawberries.

Nutritional information per portion: Energy 286kcal/1195kJ; Protein 9.1g; Carbohydrate 30.4g, of which sugars 30.4g; Fat 16.2g, of which saturates 8.9g; Cholesterol 17mg; Calcium 217mg; Fibre 2.2g; Sodium 93mg.

Very berry

Fresh and frozen cranberries are often in short supply, but dried berries are available all year round and make a tasty dairy-free shake when combined with soya milk. Tiny crimson redcurrants make the perfect partner in this refreshingly tart, sparkling smoothie.

MAKES 1 LARGE GLASS

25g/1oz/¼ cup dried cranberries
150g/5oz/1¼ cups redcurrants, plus
    extra to decorate
10ml/2 tsp clear honey
50ml/2fl oz/¼ cup soya milk
sparkling mineral water

1 Put the cranberries in a small bowl, pour over 90ml/6 tbsp boiling water and leave for 10 minutes.

2 String the redcurrants by drawing the stems through the tines of a fork to pull off the delicate currants.

3 Blend the currants, cranberries and water, honey and soya milk in a food processor/blender until smooth.

4 Pour the berry shake into a large glass, then top with a little sparkling mineral water to lighten the drink. Drape the redcurrants decoratively over the edge of the glass and serve the smoothie immediately.

Nutritional information per portion: Energy 126kcal/539kJ; Protein 3.8g; Carbohydrate 27.1g, of which sugars 27.1g; Fat 1g, of which saturates 0.1g; Cholesterol 0mg; Calcium 115mg; Fibre 7g; Sodium 25mg.

Smooth and simple

A pre-packed, mixed bag of frozen summer fruits makes an unbelievably simple base for drinks. Mixed with orange juice and enriched with a tempting swirl of cream, this smoothie is made in a flash – the perfect accompaniment to a relaxing afternoon in the sunshine.

MAKES 3 GLASSES

500g/1lb 2oz frozen mixed summer fruits, partially thawed
30ml/2 tbsp caster (superfine) sugar
about 300ml/$\frac{1}{2}$ pint/1$\frac{1}{4}$ cups freshly squeezed orange juice
60ml/4 tbsp single (light) cream

1 Tip all but a few of the summer fruits into a blender or food processor and add the sugar and orange juice. Blend until smooth, adding a little more orange juice if the mixture is too thick.

2 Pour the smoothie into three tall glasses and, using a teaspoon, swirl a little cream into each glass. Top with the reserved fruits and serve with long spoons to mix in the cream.

COOK'S TIP

If you do not want to squeeze the oranges, you can buy juice – but avoid the concentrated types.

Nutritional information per portion: Energy 159kcal/669kJ; Protein 2.5g; Carbohydrate 29.7g, of which sugars 29.7g; Fat 4.1g, of which saturates 2.4g; Cholesterol 11mg; Calcium 60mg; Fibre 1.9g; Sodium 26mg.

Fruit-tea smoothie

You can use any of the many fruit teas widely available in most large supermarkets for this thick, creamy and satisfying blend. This recipe uses dried apricots and apples but you could just as easily use dried pears, peaches or tropical dried fruits.

MAKES 2 GLASSES

50g/2oz dried apples
25g/1oz dried apricots
2 fruit teabags
juice of 1 lemon
30ml/2 tbsp crème fraîche or natural
    (plain) yogurt
mineral water (optional)

1 Using a small, sharp knife, roughly chop the dried apples and apricots. Steep the teabags in 300ml/$\frac{1}{2}$ pint/1$\frac{1}{4}$ cups boiling water for 5 minutes, then remove the teabags.

2 Add the chopped fruit to the tea and leave to stand for 30 minutes. Chill in the refrigerator for about 30 minutes until the tea is completely cold.

3 Put the fruit and tea mixture into a blender or food processor and add the lemon juice. Blend well until smooth, scraping the mixture down from the side of the bowl, if necessary.

4 Add the crème fraîche or yogurt and blend briefly, adding a little mineral water if the smoothie is too thick. Serve in tall glasses.

Nutritional information per portion: Energy 116kcal/486kJ; Protein 1.9g; Carbohydrate 14.1g, of which sugars 14g; Fat 6.2g, of which saturates 4.1g; Cholesterol 17mg; Calcium 36mg; Fibre 2.4g; Sodium 9mg.

Ruby dreamer

Figs have a distinctive yet delicate taste and are best used in simple combinations, with ingredients that enhance, rather than mask, their flavour. Like most fruits, fresh figs are now available most of the year round but they are often at their best in winter when ruby oranges are also in season – giving you the perfect excuse to make this veritable treat of a smoothie.

MAKES 2 GLASSES

6 large ripe figs
4 ruby oranges
15ml/1 tbsp dark muscovado (molasses) sugar
30–45ml/2–3 tbsp lemon juice
crushed ice

1 Cut off the hard, woody tips from the stalks of the figs, then use a sharp knife to cut each fruit in half.

2 Squeeze the oranges, using a citrus juicer or by hand. Pour the juice into a blender or food processor and add the figs and sugar. Process well until the mixture is really smooth and fairly thick, scraping the fruit down from the side of the bowl, if necessary.

3 Add lemon juice and blend briefly. Pour over crushed ice and serve.

Nutritional information per portion: Energy 417kcal/1776kJ; Protein 7.2g; Carbohydrate 97.8g, of which sugars 97.8g; Fat 2.5g, of which saturates 0g; Cholesterol 0mg; Calcium 443mg; Fibre 13.8g; Sodium 96mg.

Mango mania

Even people on a dairy-free diet can enjoy rich, creamy, indulgent drinks. This one is made using soya milk, which is particularly good in milkshakes and smoothies. It has a lovely caramel flavour that blends brilliantly with fruit purées, especially those made from fruits with an intense, naturally sweet taste, such as mangoes.

MAKES 2 TALL GLASSES

1 medium mango
300ml/¹⁄₂ pint/1¹⁄₄ cups soya milk
finely grated rind and juice of 1 lime, plus
   extra rind for garnish
15–30ml/1–2 tbsp clear honey
crushed ice

1 Using a sharp knife, peel the mango and cut the flesh off the stone (pit). Place the chopped flesh in a blender or food processor and add the soya milk, lime rind and juice and a little honey. Blend until smooth and frothy.

2 Taste the mixture and add more honey, if you like, blending until well mixed. Place some crushed ice in two glasses, then pour over the smoothie. Sprinkle with lime rind and serve.

Nutritional information per portion: Energy 111kcal/468kJ; Protein 4.9g; Carbohydrate 17.1g, of which sugars 16.9g; Fat 2.6g, of which saturates 0.6g; Cholesterol 0mg; Calcium 29mg; Fibre 2g; Sodium 51mg.

Berry and oat milk smoothie

This simple recipe uses oat milk, a cholesterol-free, calcium-rich alternative to cow's milk, and a good partner to sweet summer fruits. Although a good store-cupboard stand-by, you might prefer to keep the oat milk in the refrigerator, ready for when you need it.

MAKES 2 GLASSES

250g/9oz frozen mixed summer fruits, partially thawed, plus
   extra to garnish
130g/4$^{1}/_{2}$oz/generous $^{1}/_{2}$ cup soya yogurt
45ml/3 tbsp vanilla syrup
350ml/12fl oz/1$^{1}/_{2}$ cups oat milk

1 Put the partially thawed mixed summer fruits in a blender or food processor. Add the soya yogurt and blend thoroughly to make a thick purée. Scrape the mixture down from the side of the bowl with a rubber spatula, if necessary, and blend again, briefly, to incorporate into the mixture.

2 Add the vanilla syrup and oat milk to the fruit purée and blend the mixture again until smooth.

3 Transfer the smoothie to a small jug (pitcher) and chill, or pour it into two tall glasses and serve immediately, decorated with the extra fruits.

Nutritional information per portion: Energy 204kcal/856kJ; Protein 9.4g; Carbohydrate 29.2g, of which sugars 29.2g; Fat 4.1g, of which saturates 0.9g; Cholesterol 1mg; Calcium 47mg; Fibre 1.4g; Sodium 125mg.

Pear, rhubarb and cranberry cooler

For best results, this delicious smoothie should be made with really ripe and extremely juicy pears, so leave hard ones to ripen for several days before making this fresh and fruity treat. Also, cook the rhubarb well in advance to give it plenty of time to cool before blending.

MAKES 3–4 GLASSES

400g/14oz early rhubarb
2 large ripe pears
130g/4$^{1}/_{2}$oz/generous 1 cup fresh or
   frozen cranberries
90g/3$^{1}/_{2}$oz/$^{1}/_{2}$ cup caster (superfine) sugar
mineral water (optional)

1 Using a small, sharp knife, trim the rhubarb and cut into 2cm/$^{3}/_{4}$in lengths.

2 Place the rhubarb slices in a pan with 90ml/6 tbsp water and cover with a tight-fitting lid. Cook gently for about 5 minutes or until tender. Transfer to a bowl and leave to cool, putting several pieces aside for garnish.

3 Peel, quarter and core the pears and tip into a blender or food processor with the cranberries, the rhubarb and its cooking juices and the sugar.

4 Blend until smooth, scraping down the side of the bowl, if necessary. Thin with mineral water, if you like, then serve, garnished with the rhubarb pieces.

Nutritional information per portion: Energy 138kcal/590kJ; Protein 1.4g; Carbohydrate 34.9g, of which sugars 34.9g; Fat 0.2g, of which saturates 0g; Cholesterol 0mg; Calcium 115mg; Fibre 3.6g; Sodium 7mg.

Honey and banana milkshake

This delicious drink proves just how good a milkshake can be, even without dairy produce. Together, soya or rice milk and an iced vanilla-flavoured, non-dairy dessert produce a surprisingly rich and creamy flavour. With added bananas, this is almost a meal in itself.

MAKES 2 GLASSES

2 bananas
30ml/2 tbsp clear honey
15ml/1 tbsp lemon juice
**300ml/¹⁄₂ pint/1¹⁄₄ cups soya or
    rice milk**
4 scoops vanilla iced non-dairy dessert

1 Blend the bananas, in pieces, with the honey and lemon juice in a blender or food processor until very smooth. Scrape the mixture down from the side of the bowl with a rubber spatula, if necessary.

2 Add the soya or rice milk and two scoops of iced non-dairy dessert, then blend until smooth. Pour into tall glasses and add another scoop of dessert to each. Serve immediately.

Nutritional information per portion: Energy 416kcal/1749kJ; Protein 6.1g; Carbohydrate 68.4g, of which sugars 65.6g; Fat 15g, of which saturates 8.9g; Cholesterol 10mg; Calcium 117mg; Fibre 2.3g; Sodium 81mg.

Real vanilla milkshake

This is a milkshake for connoisseurs: it is the cream of the crop and definitely one to linger over. Nothing beats the flavour achieved by infusing a vanilla pod in the milk beforehand, but if you just cannot wait for the milk to cool, use a teaspoon of good-quality vanilla essence instead.

MAKES 2 GLASSES

1 vanilla pod (bean)
400ml/14fl oz/1²/₃ cups full cream (whole) milk
200ml/7fl oz/scant 1 cup single (light) cream
4 scoops vanilla ice cream

1 Using a sharp knife, score the vanilla pod down the centre. Place in a small pan, pour the milk over and bring slowly to the boil.

2 Remove the pan from the heat but leave the pod in the milk. Leave to stand until the milk has cooled.

3 Remove the vanilla pod from the cooled milk and scrape out

the seeds with the tip of a knife. Put the seeds in a blender or food processor with the milk and cream. Blend until thoroughly combined.

4 Add the vanilla ice cream to the mixture and blend well until it is deliciously thick and frothy. Pour the smoothie into two large glasses and serve immediately with stirrers and straws to decorate, if you like.

Nutritional information per portion: Energy 648kcal/2687kJ; Protein 15.8g; Carbohydrate 36.4g, of which sugars 36.3g; Fat 49.6g, of which saturates 30.8g; Cholesterol 83mg; Calcium 475mg; Fibre 0g; Sodium 205mg.

Rosemary nectar

This is one of those smoothies that's only worth making with perfect, ripe ingredients. The fabulous fragrance of fresh rosemary reacts with the sweet, scented flavour of juicy nectarines to produce a mouthwatering taste that will almost explode on your tongue.

MAKES 3 GLASSES

4 long rosemary sprigs, plus extra
    to decorate
15ml/1 tbsp golden caster (superfine)
    sugar
2.5ml/¹/₂ tsp ground ginger
2 oranges
4 nectarines
ice cubes

1 Put the rosemary sprigs in a small pan with the sugar, ground ginger and 150ml/¹/₄ pint/²/₃ cup water. Heat gently until the sugar dissolves, then simmer for 1 minute. Remove from the heat, transfer the sprigs and syrup to a bowl and leave to cool.

2 Squeeze the oranges. Halve and stone (pit) the nectarines and put in a food processor or blender with the orange juice. Process until smooth but don't worry if there are a few specks of nectarine skin dotting the juice.

3 Remove the rosemary from the syrup and pour into the juice. Blend briefly.

4 Put a few ice cubes in each glass and fill with the juice. Serve immediately, with extra rosemary sprigs to decorate.

Nutritional information per portion: Energy 123kcal/527kJ; Protein 3.5g; Carbohydrate 28.7g, of which sugars 28.7g; Fat 0.3g, of which saturates 0g; Cholesterol 0mg; Calcium 61mg; Fibre 3.7g; Sodium 7mg.

Vanilla snow

While a good quality vanilla essence is perfectly acceptable for flavouring drinks, a far more aromatic taste will be achieved using a vanilla pod. This simple smoothie is deliciously scented, creamy and thick, and well worth the extravagance of using a whole vanilla pod.

MAKES 3 GLASSES

1 vanilla pod (bean)
25g/1oz/2 tbsp caster (superfine) sugar
3 eating apples
300g/11oz/1¹⁄₃ cups natural (plain) yogurt

1 With a knife, split open the vanilla pod lengthways. Put it in a small pan with the sugar and 75ml/5 tbsp water. Heat until the sugar dissolves, then boil for 1 minute. Remove from the heat and leave to steep for 10 minutes.

2 Cut the apples into large chunks and push through the juicer, then pour the juice into a large bowl or jug (pitcher).

3 Lift the vanilla pod out of the pan and scrape the tiny black seeds back into the syrup. Pour into the apple juice.

4 Add the yogurt to the bowl or jug and whisk well by hand or with an electric mixer until thick and frothy. Pour into glasses and serve.

Nutritional information per portion: Energy 124kcal/527kJ; Protein 5.4g; Carbohydrate 25.1g, of which sugars 25.1g; Fat 1.1g, of which saturates 0.5g; Cholesterol 1mg; Calcium 198mg; Fibre 1.6g; Sodium 86mg.

Raspberry, apple and rose water smoothie

Although usually put through the juicer for drinking, apples can be blended as long as you process them well for a flavour-packed smoothie. Then thin with fresh apple juice – either shop-bought or home-made.

MAKES 2 GLASSES

2 eating apples
10ml/2 tsp caster (superfine) sugar
15ml/1 tbsp lemon juice
130g/4¹/₂oz/³/₄ cup fresh or frozen raspberries
150ml/¹/₄ pint/²/₃ cup apple juice
15–30ml/1–2 tbsp rose water
whole raspberries and rose petals, to decorate (optional)

1 Peel and core the apples and put in a blender or food processor with the sugar and lemon juice. Blend well until smooth, scraping the mixture down from the side of the bowl, if necessary.

2 Add the raspberries and apple juice to the apple purée and blend until completely smooth.

3 Add the rose water to the smoothie and blend briefly to combine.

4 Pour the smoothie into two medium glasses and place whole raspberries and rose petals on top of the drinks to decorate, if you like. Serve the smoothie immediately, or chill in the refrigerator until ready to serve.

Nutritional information per portion: Energy 91kcal/391kJ; Protein 1.3g; Carbohydrate 22.3g, of which sugars 22.3g; Fat 0.4g, of which saturates 0.1g; Cholesterol 0mg; Calcium 27mg; Fibre 2.9g; Sodium 6mg.

Coconut and hazelnut smoothie

This intensely nutty, rich and creamy drink is one to sip at your leisure. Leftovers can be put in the refrigerator for up to a couple of days, in which time the flavour of the hazelnuts will develop.

MAKES 2 GLASSES

90g/3¹/₂oz/scant 1 cup whole blanched hazelnuts
25g/1oz/2 tbsp golden caster (superfine) sugar
2.5ml/¹/₂ tsp almond essence (extract)
200ml/7fl oz/scant 1 cup coconut cream
30ml/2 tbsp double (heavy) cream (optional)
150ml/¹/₄ pint/²/₃ cup mineral water
crushed ice

1 Roughly chop the hazelnuts and lightly toast them in a small frying pan, turning frequently. Leave to cool, then tip the nuts into a blender or food processor with the caster sugar and blend well until very finely ground.

2 Add the almond essence, coconut cream and double cream, if using, and blend thoroughly until smooth.

3 Strain the mixture through a sieve (strainer) into a jug (pitcher), pressing down hard with the back of a spoon to get as much juice as possible. Stir in the mineral water.

4 Half-fill two glasses with crushed ice and pour over the nut smoothie. Serve the drinks immediately, or chill in the refrigerator until ready to serve.

Nutritional information per portion: Energy 364kcal/1514kJ; Protein 6.7g; Carbohydrate 20.7g, of which sugars 19.8g; Fat 28.9g, of which saturates 2.3g; Cholesterol 0mg; Calcium 99mg; Fibre 2.9g; Sodium 114mg.

Purple haze

Thick, dark blueberry purée swirled into pale and creamy vanilla-flavoured buttermilk looks stunning and tastes simply divine. Despite its creaminess, the buttermilk gives this sumptuous smoothie a delicious sharp tang.

MAKES 2 TALL GLASSES

250g/9oz/2¼ cups blueberries

50g/2oz/¼ cup caster (superfine) sugar

15ml/1 tbsp lemon juice

300ml/½ pint/1¼ cups buttermilk

5ml/1 tsp vanilla essence (extract)

150ml/¼ pint/⅔ cup full cream (whole) milk

1 Push the blueberries through a juicer and stir in 15ml/1 tbsp of the sugar and the lemon juice. Stir well and divide between two tall glasses.

2 Put the buttermilk, vanilla essence, milk and remaining sugar in a blender or food processor and blend until really frothy. Alternatively, use a hand-held electric blender and blend until the mixture froths up. If you do not like buttermilk, use half natural yogurt and half milk instead.

3 Pour the buttermilk mixture over the blueberry juice so the mixtures swirl together naturally – there is no need to stir them together as it tastes and looks better if they remain separate to a certain degree. Serve immediately.

Nutritional information per portion: Energy 274kcal/1157kJ; Protein 9.1g; Carbohydrate 54.2g, of which sugars 49.2g; Fat 3.9g, of which saturates 2.4g; Cholesterol 13mg; Calcium 284mg; Fibre 2.5g; Sodium 99mg.

Lemon meringue

Just as lemon meringue pie is a favourite dessert, this wonderful milkshake is sure to become a favourite drink. The blend of sweet meringue and lemon is carefully balanced in a velvety smooth, ice-cool drink that is not too rich and surprisingly refreshing.

MAKES 2 GLASSES

30ml/2 tbsp caster (superfine) sugar
3 lemons
50g/2oz crisp white meringues
300ml/¹/₂ pint/¹/₄ cups full cream (whole) milk
2 scoops vanilla ice cream
lemon slices or twists of peel, to decorate

1 Put the sugar in a small pan with 100ml/3¹/₂fl oz/scant ¹/₂ cup water and heat gently until the sugar dissolves. Pour into a jug (pitcher). Squeeze the lemons using a citrus juicer and add the juice to the syrup. Leave to cool.

2 Coarsely crush 15g/¹/₂oz of the meringues and reserve for decoration. Break the remainder into a food processor. Add the lemon syrup and blend until smooth.

3 With the machine still running, gradually pour in the milk until the mixture is pale and frothy. Add the ice cream and blend again until smooth.

4 Pour the milkshake into tall glasses and decorate the sides with lemon slices or twists of lemon peel. Scatter the reserved meringue on top and serve.

Nutritional information per portion:Energy 331kcal/1398kJ; Protein 8.5g; Carbohydrate 55.2g, of which sugars 55.1g; Fat 10.1g, of which saturates 6.2g; Cholesterol 9mg; Calcium 241mg; Fibre 0g; Sodium 125mg.

Rose petal and almond milk

If you're lucky enough to have a mass of roses in the garden, it's worth sacrificing a few for this delicately scented summer smoothie. Thickened and flavoured with ground ratafia biscuits, this fragrant drink is the perfect way to relax on a hot lazy afternoon.

MAKES 2 GLASSES

15g/½oz scented rose petals (preferably pink), plus extra
   to decorate
300ml/½ pint/1¼ cups milk
25g/1oz ratafia biscuits (almond macaroons)
ice cubes

1 Put the rose petals in a small pan with half the milk and bring just to the boil. Put the ratafia biscuits in a bowl, pour over the hot milk and leave to stand for 10 minutes.

2 Transfer the mixture to a blender or food processor with the remaining milk, and blend until smooth.

3 Strain the milk through a sieve (strainer) into a wide jug (pitcher) to remove any lumps of biscuit or rose petals that have not been blended properly, and chill for at least 1 hour.

4 When the milk is well chilled, pour over ice cubes and serve immediately, decorating with rose petals, if you like.

Nutritional information per portion: Energy 124kcal/523kJ; Protein 5.8g; Carbohydrate 17g, of which sugars 11.5g; Fat 4.2g, of which saturates 2.4g; Cholesterol 9mg; Calcium 197mg; Fibre 0.2g; Sodium 106mg.

Banana and maple crunch

Brilliant for making quick and easy blended drinks, bananas perfectly complement maple syrup and pecan nuts. Serve this creamy, syrupy smoothie over ice and, if you are feeling decadent, dunk in some chunky chocolate cookies to scoop up a mouthful.

MAKES 2 GLASSES

2 large bananas
50g/2oz/½ cup pecan nuts, plus extra to serve
150ml/¼ pint/⅔ cup full cream (whole) milk
60ml/4 tbsp pure maple syrup
crushed ice

1 Put the bananas in a blender or food processor and process until smooth. Add the nuts and blend again until thoroughly combined.

2 The nuts must be finely ground so stop and scrape down the side of the bowl once or twice, if necessary.

3 Add the maple syrup, then pour the milk over the banana paste and blend again until creamy.

4 Half-fill two large glasses with crushed ice and pour the smoothie over the top. Serve sprinkled with extra pecan nuts, if you like.

Nutritional information per portion: Energy 391kcal/1641kJ; Protein 6.2g; Carbohydrate 51.9g, of which sugars 49.2g; Fat 19.1g, of which saturates 2.4g; Cholesterol 4mg; Calcium 116mg; Fibre 2.3g; Sodium 115mg.

Cinnamon squash

Lightly cooked butternut squash has a wonderfully rich, rounded flavour that is lifted perfectly by tart citrus juice and warm, spicy cinnamon. Imagine pumpkin pie as a gorgeous smooth drink and you're halfway to experiencing the flavours of this lusciously sweet and tantalizing treat.

MAKES 2–3 GLASSES

1 small butternut squash, about 600g/
    1lb 6oz
2.5ml/½ tsp ground cinnamon
3 large lemons
1 grapefruit
60ml/4 tbsp light muscovado (brown)
    sugar
ice cubes

1 Halve the squash, scoop out and discard the seeds and cut the flesh into chunks. Cut away the skin and discard. Steam or boil the squash for 10–15 minutes until just tender. Drain well and leave to stand until cool.

2 Put the cooled squash in a blender or food processor and add the ground cinnamon.

3 Squeeze the lemons and grapefruit and pour the juice over the squash, then add the muscovado sugar.

4 Process the ingredients until they are very smooth. If necessary, pause to scrape down the side of the food processor or blender. Serve immediately in short glasses over ice cubes.

Nutritional information per portion: Energy 121kcal/513kJ; Protein 1.9g; Carbohydrate 28.9g, of which sugars 27.9g; Fat 0.5g, of which saturates 0.2g; Cholesterol 0mg; Calcium 81mg; Fibre 2.7g; Sodium 3mg.

Green devil

Choose a well-flavoured avocado, such as a knobbly, dark-skinned Haas, for this slightly spicy, hot and sour smoothie. Cucumber adds a refreshing edge, while lemon and lime juice zip up the flavour, and the chilli sauce adds an irresistible fiery bite.

MAKES 2–3 GLASSES

1 small ripe avocado
¹/₂ cucumber
30ml/2 tbsp lemon juice
30ml/2 tbsp lime juice
10ml/2 tsp caster (superfine) sugar
pinch of salt
**250ml/8fl oz/1 cup apple juice or
    mineral water**
10–20ml/2–4 tsp sweet chilli sauce
ice cubes
red chilli curls, to decorate

1 Halve the avocado and use a sharp knife to remove the stone (pit). Scoop the flesh from both halves into a blender or food processor. Peel and roughly chop the cucumber and add to the blender or food processor, then add the lemon and lime juice, the caster sugar and a little salt.

2 Process the ingredients until smooth and creamy, then add the apple juice or mineral water and a little of the chilli sauce. Blend once more to lightly mix the ingredients together.

3 Pour the smoothie over ice cubes. Decorate with red chilli curls and serve with stirrers and extra chilli sauce.

Nutritional information per portion: Energy 143kcal/598kJ; Protein 1.3g; Carbohydrate 13.2g, of which sugars 12.5g; Fat 9.8g, of which saturates 2.1g; Cholesterol 0mg; Calcium 19mg; Fibre 1.9g; Sodium 6mg.

Rosemary and almond cream

This delightful concoction is definitely one to choose if you are looking for something a little different. Fresh sprigs of rosemary, infused in milk, provide a gentle fragrance and flavour that blends deliciously with the sweet ratafia biscuits.

MAKES 2 GLASSES

4 long sprigs of fresh rosemary
400ml/14fl oz/1²/₃ cups full cream (whole) milk
50g/2oz ratafia biscuits (almond macaroons) or amaretti, plus extra to decorate
3 large scoops vanilla ice cream
frosted rosemary sprigs, to decorate

1 Put the rosemary sprigs in a small pan. Add 150ml/ ¹/₄ pint/²/₃ cup of the milk and heat very gently until the milk begins to boil. Remove the pan from the heat and tip the mixture into a bowl. Leave to cool for 10 minutes.

2 Remove the rosemary sprigs and carefully pour the still warm milk into a blender or food processor. Add the ratafia biscuits and blend until smooth and creamy. Add the remaining 250ml/8fl oz/1 cup milk and blend the mixture thoroughly.

3 Scoop the vanilla ice cream into the milk and biscuit mixture and blend until it is fully incorporated. Pour into large glasses and serve the milkshake immediately, decorating the top of each glass with delicate frosted rosemary sprigs and a few pieces of crumbled ratafia biscuits.

Nutritional information per portion: Energy 400kcal/1684kJ; Protein 12.3g; Carbohydrate 51.5g, of which sugars 39.4g; Fat 16.4g, of which saturates 10.5g; Cholesterol 39mg; Calcium 385mg; Fibre 0.4g; Sodium 236mg.

Pistachio thick-shake

Don't be put off by the presence of rice in this lovely, layered dairy-free milkshake. Blended with soya milk, pistachio nuts and non-dairy ice cream, it makes a dreamy, creamy blend that can be sipped, layer by layer, or swirled together with a pretty stirrer.

MAKES 3–4 GLASSES

550ml/18fl oz/2¹/₂ cups soya milk
50g/2oz/generous ¹/₄ cup pudding rice
60ml/4 tbsp caster (superfine) sugar
finely grated rind of 1 lemon
75g/3oz/³/₄ cup shelled pistachio nuts, plus extra to decorate
300ml/10fl oz vanilla iced non-dairy dessert
5ml/1 tsp almond essence (extract)

1 Bring the soya milk, rice, sugar and lemon rind to the boild in a large pan, then simmer. Partially cover the pan with a lid and cook on the lowest heat until the rice is completely tender. Leave to cool in a heatproof bowl.

2 Put the pistachio nuts in another heatproof bowl and cover with boiling water. Leave for 2 minutes, then drain. Rub them between several layers of kitchen paper and peel away the skins.

3 Blend the cold rice in a blender until smooth. Put half the mixture in a bowl. Add the non-dairy dessert to the blender and blend until smooth. Pour into a separate bowl. Add the nuts, reserved rice and almond essence to the blender and process until finely ground. Layer the two mixtures in glasses. Serve decorated with pistachios.

Nutritional information per portion: Energy 397kcal/1660kJ; Protein 11.4g; Carbohydrate 47.1g, of which sugars 34.1g; Fat 18.6g, of which saturates 4.8g; Cholesterol 5mg; Calcium 154mg; Fibre 1.2g; Sodium 189mg.

Rocky river

This rich, sweet milkshake combines chilled custard with decadent chocolate, chunky nuts and delicious marshmallows. It is great fun to make with children, who will enjoy its sticky sweetness almost as much as the adults. Prepare this shake when you need a real treat.

MAKES 3 GLASSES

75g/3oz plain (semisweet) chocolate
40g/1¹/₂ oz/scant ¹/₂ cup blanched almonds
50g/2oz pink and white marshmallows
600ml/1 pint/2¹/₂ cups good quality ready-made custard
300ml/¹/₂ pint/1¹/₄ cups milk
30ml/2 tbsp caster (superfine) sugar
5ml/1 tsp vanilla essence (extract)

1 Coarsely grate the chocolate. Lightly toast the almonds, then chop them. Cut the marshmallows roughly into pieces, using scissors, reserving a few pieces for decoration.

2 Tip the custard into a blender or food processor and add the milk, sugar and vanilla essence. Blend briefly to combine.

3 Reserve a little chocolate for sprinkling, then add the remainder to the blender with the almonds and marshmallows. Blend until the marshmallows are chopped into small pieces.

4 Pour into large glasses and serve immediately, sprinkled with the reserved marshmallows and grated chocolate.

Nutritional information per portion: Energy 545kcal/2296kJ; Protein 13.6g; Carbohydrate 78.4g, of which sugars 67.7g; Fat 19.7g, of which saturates 5.9g; Cholesterol 12mg; Calcium 348mg; Fibre 1.8g; Sodium 134mg.

Chocolate brownie milkshake

For a truly indulgent flavour, use home-made chocolate brownies in this fabulously tasty milkshake. It is very rich – and incredibly decadent – so sit back, relax and just enjoy a totally luxurious moment on your own – well, you wouldn't want to share it.

MAKES 1 LARGE GLASS

40g/1¹/₂oz chocolate brownies
200ml/7fl oz/scant 1 cup full cream (whole) milk
2 scoops vanilla ice cream
a little whipped cream
chocolate shavings or cocoa powder (unsweetened), to decorate

1 Crumble the chocolate brownies into a blender or food processor and add the milk. Blend until the mixture is a pale chocolate colour.

2 Add the ice cream and blend until smooth and frothy. Pour into a tall glass and spoon over a little whipped cream. Serve scattered with chocolate shavings or a dusting of cocoa powder.

COOK'S TIP
If you fancy treating yourself to a milkshake that's even more chocolatey than this one, replace the vanilla ice cream with the same amount of a chocolate or chocolate-chip variety.

Nutritional information per portion: Energy 637kcal/2652kJ; Protein 15.4g; Carbohydrate 54.4g, of which sugars 45.5g; Fat 41g, of which saturates 18.6g; Cholesterol 28mg; Calcium 416mg; Fibre 0g; Sodium 348mg.

Marzipan and orange crush

The wintry scents and flavours of juicy oranges and marzipan make an interesting combination, while the citrus juice adds a delicious refreshing tang to an otherwise very rich, creamy drink. It's a great blend to make if you are entertaining friends.

MAKES 3–4 GLASSES

130g/4^1/$_2$oz marzipan
finely grated rind and juice of 2 large oranges
juice of 1 lemon
150ml/^{1}/$_4$ pint/^{2}/$_3$ cup mineral water
150ml/^{1}/$_4$ pint/^{2}/$_3$ cup single (light) cream
ice cubes
orange wedges, to decorate (optional)

1 Break the marzipan into small pieces and put in a blender or food processor. Add the orange rind and juice along with the lemon juice. Blend the mixture thoroughly until smooth.

2 Add the mineral water and cream and blend again until smooth and frothy. Pour over ice cubes in glasses and serve decorated with the orange wedges, if you like.

COOK'S TIP
It's a good idea to give this drink a whisk before serving, as it may have settled.

Nutritional information per portion: Energy 208kcal/871kJ; Protein 3.1g; Carbohydrate 25g, of which sugars 25g; Fat 11.3g, of which saturates 4.9g; Cholesterol 21mg; Calcium 57mg; Fibre 0.7g; Sodium 20mg.

Cherry and coconut shake

The season for fresh cherries is all too short, but canned cherries are a surprisingly good stand-by. Here, they combine in a classic partnership with creamy coconut milk to make a fruity drink that is perfect for people who are not too keen on really sweet, thick milkshakes.

MAKES 2 GLASSES

425g/15oz can pitted black cherries in syrup
200ml/7fl oz/scant 1 cup coconut milk
15ml/1 tbsp light muscovado (brown) sugar
150ml/^{1}/$_4$ pint/^{2}/$_3$ cup black cherry-flavour yogurt
100ml/3^1/$_2$fl oz/scant ^{1}/$_2$ cup double (heavy) cream
lightly toasted shredded coconut, to decorate

1 Tip the canned cherries into a sieve (strainer) over a bowl to drain. Reserve the syrup for later.

2 Put the drained cherries in a blender or food processor with the coconut milk and sugar and blend briefly until fairly smooth. (Do not be tempted to over-blend the mixture or it may begin to separate.)

3 Pour the mixture through a sieve into a jug (pitcher), pressing the pulp down into the sieve with the back of a spoon to extract as much juice as possible.

4 Add the reserved cherry syrup, yogurt and cream and whisk lightly until smooth and frothy. Pour into glasses and scatter with shredded coconut.

Nutritional information per portion: Energy 518kcal/2176kJ; Protein 5.3g; Carbohydrate 66.4g, of which sugars 66.4g; Fat 27.7g, of which saturates 17.2g; Cholesterol 72mg; Calcium 202mg; Fibre 1.3g; Sodium 187mg.

Drinks for kids

With these delicious recipes, you can add some extra zing to breakfast and after-school drinks, and liven up kids' parties. There are fresh fruit squashes, fun fizzes and shakes, and some real teatime treats that could quite easily take the place of an ordinary dessert or pudding. Let the kids help prepare them and they'll enjoy these blends even more.

Top pops

Chunky ice-lolly stirrers make this fruit-packed smoothie very appealing to children. It's great for a party or as an after-school treat on a hot day. The lollies can be frozen ahead and stored so they're ready on demand, and the juice takes just moments to prepare.

MAKES 2 GLASSES

1 apple
300ml/¹⁄₂ pint/1¹⁄₄ cups apple juice
2 kiwi fruit
90g/3¹⁄₂oz/generous ¹⁄₂ cup raspberries
10ml/2 tsp caster (superfine) sugar
150g/5oz/1 cup red grapes
150g/5oz/1¹⁄₄ cups blackcurrants or
   blackberries
1 large banana

1 Peel, core and roughly chop the apple. Place in a food processor or blender with 100ml/3¹⁄₂fl oz/ scant ¹⁄₂ cup of the apple juice and blend to a smooth purée. Pour into a third of the sections of an ice-cube tray.

2 Peel and roughly chop the kiwi fruit and then blend until smooth with 100ml of the apple juice. Pour into another third of the ice-cube tray sections.

3 Blend the raspberries with the sugar and the remaining apple juice and spoon into the final sections. Freeze the tray for about 30 minutes then push a wooden ice-lolly (popsicle) stick into each. Freeze until solid.

4 Blend the grapes, blackcurrants (or blackberries) and banana in a blender or food processor until smooth. If you like, push the mixture through a coarse strainer after blending to remove the seeds and skins.

5 Push several of the fruit lollies out of the tray and place on separate plates for each child. Pour the fruit juice into two glasses and place on plates with the lollies. Serve immediately as the lollies will start to melt very quickly – and don't forget to supply the children with plenty of napkins.

Nutritional information per portion: Energy 231kcal/986kJ; Protein 3g; Carbohydrate 56.2g, of which sugars 55.1g; Fat 1g, of which saturates 0.1g; Cholesterol 0mg; Calcium 84mg; Fibre 6.1g; Sodium 11mg.

Tropical fruit shake

Sweet, fruity and packed with vitamin C, this is a brilliant way to get children to enjoy healthy drinks. If you use really ripe fruit, it shouldn't need any additional sweetening, but taste it before serving. Mango makes a thick purée when blended, so top it up with mineral water.

MAKES 2 GLASSES

1/2 **small pineapple**
small bunch seedless white grapes
1 mango
mineral water or lemonade (optional)

1 Using a sharp knife, cut away the skin from the pineapple and halve the fruit. Discard the core and roughly chop the flesh of one half. Add to a blender or food processor with the grapes. Halve the mango either side of the flat stone (pit). Scoop the flesh into the blender.

2 Process thoroughly until really smooth, scraping the mixture down from the side of the bowl, if necessary. Pour into glasses and top up with mineral water or lemonade, if using. Serve immediately.

Nutritional information per portion: Energy 129kcal/553kJ; Protein 1.3g; Carbohydrate 32.3g, of which sugars 32g; Fat 0.4g, of which saturates 0.1g; Cholesterol 0mg; Calcium 37mg; Fibre 3.7g; Sodium 5mg.

Puppy love

Children of all ages enjoy this semi-frozen fruit treat. Make the fruit syrup and freeze it for an hour or two so that it is ready to blend to a slushy consistency. If you forget about it and it freezes solid, let it thaw a little at room temperature or microwave for a few seconds.

MAKES 2–3 GLASSES

2 oranges
250g/9oz/2¼ cups blueberries
50g/2oz/4 tbsp caster (superfine) sugar

1 Using a small, sharp knife, carefully cut away the majority of the skin from the oranges, then cut the oranges into 8–10 chunky wedges of roughly the same size.

2 Reserve a few blueberries for decoration, then push the rest through a juicer, alternating them with the orange wedges.

3 Add the sugar and 300ml/½ pint/1¼ cups cold water to the juice and stir until the sugar has dissolved. Pour into a shallow, non-metallic freezer container and freeze for 1–2 hours or until the juice is beginning to freeze all over.

4 Use a fork to break up any solid areas of the mixture and tip into a blender or food processor. Blend until smooth and slushy. Spoon the drink into glasses and serve, topped with blueberries or other fruit.

Nutritional information per portion: Energy 150kcal/637kJ; Protein 2g; Carbohydrate 37.6g, of which sugars 34.3g; Fat 0.1g, of which saturates 0g; Cholesterol 0mg; Calcium 56mg; Fibre 3.4g; Sodium 6mg.

Rainbow juice

Brightly coloured layers of pure fruit juice give this smoothie extra child appeal. Strawberry, kiwi fruit and pineapple provide plenty of colour contrast but you can use almost any other fruits that blend to a fairly thick consistency, and create your own rainbow.

MAKES 3 GLASSES

4 kiwi fruit
½ small pineapple
130g/4½oz/generous 1 cup strawberries

1 Using a sharp knife, peel the kiwi fruit. Cut away the skin from the pineapple, then halve and remove the core. Roughly chop the pineapple flesh.

2 Put the pineapple in a blender or food processor and add 30ml/2 tbsp water. Process to a smooth purée, scraping the mixture down from the side of the bowl with a rubber spatula, if necessary. Tip into a small bowl.

3 Add the kiwi fruit to the blender and blend until smooth. Tip into a separate bowl. Finally, blend the strawberries until smooth.

4 Pour the strawberry purée into three glass tumblers. Carefully spoon the kiwi fruit purée into the glasses to form a separate layer. Spoon the pineapple purée over the kiwi fruit and serve with spoons or thick straws.

Nutritional information per portion: Energy 78kcal/332kJ; Protein 1.5g; Carbohydrate 17.8g, of which sugars 17.6g; Fat 0.6g, of which saturates 0g; Cholesterol 0mg; Calcium 39mg; Fibre 2.8g; Sodium 7mg.

Ruby red lemonade

Use blackberries or blueberries, or a mixture of both, in this quick and easy fruit cordial. A far healthier alternative to ready-made drinks, it's made in minutes and can be kept in the refrigerator for several days. If you have a glut of summer fruits, it makes sense to prepare extra and freeze it, preferably in single portions in ice-cube trays.

MAKES ABOUT 350ML/12FL OZ/1¹/₂ CUPS, BEFORE DILUTING

350g/12oz/3 cups blackberries or
   blueberries
130g/4¹/₂oz/scant ³/₄ cup golden caster
   (superfine) sugar
ice cubes
sparkling mineral water, to serve

1 Remove any tough stalks or leaves from the blackberries or blueberries, and then wash them thoroughly. Allow the fruit to dry.

2 Push handfuls of the fruit through a juicer.

3 Put the sugar in a small, heavy pan with 100ml/3¹/₂fl oz/scant ¹/₂ cup water. Heat gently until the sugar dissolves, stirring with a wooden spoon, then bring to the boil and boil for 3 minutes until syrupy. Reserve until cool.

4 Mix the fruit juice with the syrup in a jug (pitcher). For each serving pour about 50ml/2fl oz/¹/₄ cup fruit syrup into a tumbler and add ice. Serve topped up with sparkling mineral water.

Nutritional information per portion: Energy 712kcal/3020kJ; Protein 4.2g; Carbohydrate 184.8g, of which sugars 170.8g; Fat 0g, of which saturates 0g; Cholesterol 0mg; Calcium 69mg; Fibre 7g; Sodium 8mg.

Lemon float

Old-fashioned lemonade made with freshly squeezed lemons is a far cry from the carbonated, synthetic commercial varieties. Served with generous scoops of ice cream and soda water, it makes the ultimate refreshing dessert drink. The lemonade can be stored in the refrigerator for up to two weeks, so it is well worth making a double batch.

MAKES 4 LARGE GLASSES

6 lemons, plus wafer-thin lemon slices,
   to decorate
200g/7oz/1 cup caster (superfine) sugar
8 scoops vanilla ice cream
soda water (club soda)

1 Finely grate the rind from the lemons, then squeeze out the juice using a citrus juicer or by hand.

2 Put the rind in a bowl with the sugar and pour over 600ml/1 pint/ 2½ cups boiling water. Stir until the sugar dissolves, then leave to cool.

3 Stir in the lemon juice. Strain into a jug (pitcher) and chill for several hours.

4 Put a scoop of the vanilla ice cream in each of the glasses, then half-fill with the lemonade and add plenty of lemon slices to decorate. Top up each glass with soda water, add another scoop of ice cream to each one and serve immediately with long-handled spoons.

Nutritional information per portion: Energy 520kcal/2182kJ; Protein 6.1g; Carbohydrate 77.5g, of which sugars 77.3g; Fat 22.7g, of which saturates 13.6g; Cholesterol 0mg; Calcium 177mg; Fibre 0g; Sodium 93mg.

Custard cream float

This fabulously frothy dessert drink makes a wonderful treat that rounds off any meal brilliantly, or you could serve it to your children as a special mid-morning snack or teatime treat.

MAKES 3 GLASSES

75g/3oz custard cream biscuits (cookies)
1 large banana
5ml/1 tsp vanilla essence (extract)
200ml/7fl oz/scant 1 cup full cream (whole) milk
6 scoops vanilla ice cream
banana slices and crumbled biscuit (cookie), to decorate
drinking chocolate or cocoa powder (unsweetened), for dusting

1 Put the custard cream biscuits in a blender or food processor and blend well until finely ground. Break the banana into chunks and add to the ground biscuits. Process thoroughly until a smooth, thick paste forms, scraping down the side of the bowl with a rubber spatula, if necessary.

2 Add the vanilla essence, milk and three scoops of the ice cream and process again until smooth and foamy. Pour into tumblers and top with the remaining scoops of ice cream. Decorate with banana slices and crumbled biscuit and serve dusted with a little drinking chocolate or cocoa powder.

COOK'S TIP
For an extra burst of banana flavour, use banana ice cream.

Nutritional information per portion: Energy 485kcal/2027kJ; Protein 9.7g; Carbohydrate 55.7g, of which sugars 41.3g; Fat 26.2g, of which saturates 15.4g; Cholesterol 17mg; Calcium 245mg; Fibre 1g; Sodium 212mg.

Chocolate nut swirl

Children everywhere will adore this fabulous chocolatey concoction. It is a mixture of melted milk chocolate, chocolate nut spread and creamy milk, marbled together to make an attractive and delicious drink.

MAKES 2 TALL GLASSES

40g/1½oz/3 tbsp chocolate hazelnut spread
400ml/14fl oz/1²/₃ cups full cream (whole) milk
90g/3½oz milk chocolate
30ml/2 tbsp extra thick double (heavy) cream (optional)
a little crushed ice
2 chocolate flake bars, to serve

1 Put the chocolate spread in a small bowl with 10ml/2 tsp of the milk. Stir well until smooth and glossy.

2 Chop the chocolate. Put 100ml/3½fl oz/scant ½ cup of the remaining milk in a small pan and add the chocolate pieces. Heat gently, stirring until the chocolate has melted. Remove from the heat and pour into a jug (pitcher). Leave to cool for 10 minutes, then stir in the remaining milk.

3 Using a teaspoon, dot the chocolate hazelnut mixture around the sides of two tall glasses, rotating them so that each glass is randomly streaked with chocolate. Dot the cream around the glasses in the same way, if using.

4 Put a little crushed ice in each glass and pour over the chocolate milk. Serve immediately with flake bar stirrers that can be used to swirl the hazelnut mixture into the chocolate milk.

Nutritional information per portion: Energy 476kcal/1987kJ; Protein 11.3g; Carbohydrate 46.7g, of which sugars 46.6g; Fat 28.2g, of which saturates 15.3g; Cholesterol 39mg; Calcium 361mg; Fibre 0.5g; Sodium 135mg.

Raspberry rippler

Colourful ripples of raspberry and mango give instant child appeal to this fruit-packed smoothie. Soya milk is delicious and a healthy alternative to cow's milk. Here, it is blended with mango to create a smooth, thick contrast to the tangy raspberries. Try to use only really ripe, sweet mango.

MAKES 2 GLASSES

90g/3¹/₂oz/generous ¹/₂ cup fresh or frozen raspberries, plus a few extra to decorate
15–30ml/1–2 tbsp clear honey
1 mango
100ml/3¹/₂fl oz/scant ¹/₂ cup soya milk

1 Process the raspberries in a blender or food processor until smooth. Add 15ml/1 tbsp water and 5–10ml/1–2 tsp of the honey to sweeten. Transfer to a small bowl and rinse out the blender or food processor bowl.

2 Halve the mango either side of the flat stone (pit). Scoop the flesh from the two halves and around the stone into the clean blender or food processor and process until smooth. Add the soya milk and 10–20ml/2–4 tsp honey to sweeten.

3 Pour a 2.5cm/1in layer of the mango purée into two tumblers. Then spoon half the raspberry purée on top. Add the remaining mango purée, then finish with the remaining raspberry purée. Using a teaspoon, lightly swirl the two mixtures together. Serve decorated with extra raspberries.

Nutritional information per portion: Energy 92kcal/391kJ; Protein 2.7g; Carbohydrate 18.8g, of which sugars 18.6g; Fat 1.1g, of which saturates 0.3g; Cholesterol 0mg; Calcium 27mg; Fibre 3.1g; Sodium 20mg.

Peppermint crush

The next time you see seaside rock or Christmas peppermint candy canes, buy a few sticks for this incredibly easy, fun drink. All you need to do is whizz it up with some milk and freeze until slushy, so it's ready and waiting. This shake could almost pass as a dessert, so try serving it after a meal.

MAKES 4 GLASSES

90g/3½oz pink peppermint rock
   (rock candy)
750ml/1¼ pints/3 cups full cream
   (whole) or semi-skimmed
   (low-fat) milk
a few drops of pink food colouring
   (optional)
pink candy canes, to serve

1 While the rock is still in its wrapper, hit with a rolling pin to break into small bits. (If unwrapped, put the rock in a polythene bag to crush it.) Tip the pieces into a blender or food processor.

2 Add the milk and a few drops of pink food colouring, if using, to the crushed rock and process until the rock is broken up into tiny pieces.

3 Pour the mixture into a shallow freezer container and freeze for about 2 hours or until turning slushy around the edges. Beat the mixture with a fork, breaking up the semi-frozen areas and stirring them into the centre. Re-freeze and repeat the process once or twice more until the mixture is slushy. Spoon into glasses and serve with candy cane stirrers.

Nutritional information per portion: Energy 160kcal/679kJ; Protein 6.4g; Carbohydrate 28.4g, of which sugars 28.3g; Fat 3.2g, of which saturates 2g; Cholesterol 11mg; Calcium 226mg; Fibre 0g; Sodium 86mg.

Crushes and slushes

What could be better than relaxing in the garden on a hot afternoon, enjoying an ice-cool, refreshing blend? This chapter offers a fabulous fusion of flavours, whether you prefer fat-free, refreshing slushes, such as cranberry, cinnamon and ginger, or luxurious, creamy blends with white chocolate, ice cream and hazelnuts.

Cranberry, cinnamon and ginger spritzer

Partially freezing fruit juice gives it a wonderfully slushy and refreshing texture. The perfect combination of cranberry and apple juice contributes a tart, clean flavour that's not too sweet.

MAKES 4 GLASSES

600ml/1 pint/2¹/₂ cups chilled cranberry
    juice
150ml/¹/₄ pint/²/₃ cup clear apple juice
4 cinnamon sticks
about 400ml/14fl oz/1²/₃ cups chilled
    ginger ale
a few fresh or frozen cranberries,
    to decorate

1 Pour the cranberry juice into a shallow freezer container and freeze until a thick layer of ice crystals forms around the edges. Then mash the ice with a fork and return to the freezer for a further 2–3 hours until almost solid.

2 Pour the apple juice into a small pan, add two cinnamon sticks and bring to just below boiling point. Pour into a jug (pitcher) and leave to cool; remove the cinnamon sticks and set aside. Chill the juice until it is very cold.

3 Spoon the cranberry ice into a blender. Add the apple juice and blend until slushy. Pile into cocktail glasses, top up with ginger ale and decorate with the fresh or frozen cranberries. Pop a long cinnamon stick into each glass to use as a swizzle stick.

Nutritional information per portion: Energy 86kcal/370kJ; Protein 0.2g; Carbohydrate 22.5g, of which sugars 22.5g; Fat 0.2g, of which saturates 0g; Cholesterol 0mg; Calcium 13mg; Fibre 0g; Sodium 4mg.

Frosty fruits

Long after summer is over, you can still summon up the flavours of the season with this purple, slushy delight from frozen summer fruits, which will pep up even the darkest winter mornings.

MAKES 2–3 GLASSES

250g/9oz/2 cups frozen summer fruits,
    plus extra to decorate
200g/7oz/scant 1 cup natural (plain)
    yogurt
45ml/3 tbsp double (heavy) cream
30–45ml/2–3 tbsp caster (superfine)
    sugar

1 Take the frozen fruits straight from the freezer and tip them into a blender or food processor. Blend until finely crushed, scraping down the side of the bowl, if necessary.

2 Add the yogurt and cream to the crushed fruit, then spoon in 30ml/2 tbsp of the sugar. Blend again until the mixture is smooth and thick. Taste and then add the extra sugar if necessary. Serve immediately, decorated with fruit.

Nutritional information per portion: Energy
174kcal/726kJ; Protein 4.4g; Carbohydrate 20.7g,
of which sugars 20.7g; Fat 8.8g, of which saturates 5.3g;
Cholesterol 21mg; Calcium 153mg; Fibre 0.9g;
Sodium 64mg.

Strawberries and cream

Real strawberries and cream are only worth eating when fresh strawberries are at their best, and the same goes for this delectable drink. Use small, vibrantly red and thoroughly ripe fruit. Frozen whole, they serve as flavour-packed ice cubes that will chill the drink.

MAKES 2 TALL GLASSES

275g/10oz/2½ cups small strawberries
15ml/1 tbsp lemon juice
5ml/1 tsp vanilla sugar
cream soda

1 Hull the strawberries. Freeze about 130g/4½oz/ generous 1 cup of the smallest strawberries for about 1 hour, or until firm. Process the remainder in a blender or food processor with the lemon juice and sugar until smooth, scraping the mixture down from the side of the bowl, if necessary.

2 Divide the frozen strawberries between two tall glasses and pour in the strawberry purée. Top up with cream soda and serve immediately with long-handled spoons so your guests can scoop out the delicious frozen strawberries and eat them – once they have defrosted slightly.

COOK'S TIP
To make your own vanilla sugar, fill a jar with caster (superfine) sugar and press a whole vanilla pod (bean) into the centre. Seal and leave for 2–3 weeks. Top it up as you use it.

Nutritional information per portion: Energy 45kcal/189kJ; Protein 1.1g; Carbohydrate 10.4g, of which sugars 10.4g; Fat 0.2g, of which saturates 0g; Cholesterol 0mg; Calcium 23mg; Fibre 1.5g; Sodium 9mg.

Apple refresher

Made using freshly juiced apples, this vibrant blend has a wonderful crisp, thirst-quenching flavour. The really sweet, ripe fruits are juiced and then frozen until slushy. Served with more apples and topped up with sparkling water, this drink couldn't be simpler.

MAKES 3 GLASSES

6 large red eating apples
10ml/2 tsp lemon juice
a little clear honey (optional)
sparkling mineral water

1 Reserve one of the apples. Quarter and core the remainder and cut the flesh into small pieces. Juice the apple pieces and stir in the lemon juice.

2 Check for sweetness, adding a little honey, if using. (Remember that the flavour will be less sweet once frozen.) Pour into a shallow freezer container, cover and freeze until a band of slush has formed around the edges.

3 Using a fork, break up the frozen apple juice, pushing it into the centre of the container. Re-freeze for 1 hour or until slushy all over. Again, break up the mixture with a fork.

4 Quarter and core the remaining apple and cut into thin slices. Spoon the slush into three glasses until two-thirds full and tuck the apple slices down the sides. Top up with sparkling water to serve.

Nutritional information per portion: Energy 71kcal/307kJ; Protein 0.7g; Carbohydrate 18.1g, of which sugars 18.1g; Fat 0.2g, of which saturates 0g; Cholesterol 0mg; Calcium 9mg; Fibre 3.2g; Sodium 4mg.

Pineapple and yogurt ice

Cooling, delicious yogurt ice comes in several flavours, including vanilla, orange and lemon, and is the perfect, lighter summer alternative to traditional ice cream. Use a really sweet, juicy pineapple and fresh, pungent basil to add plenty of vibrant colour and exotic flavour.

MAKES 2 GLASSES

**25g/1oz fresh basil, plus extra sprigs
    to decorate**
1 pineapple
**4 large scoops vanilla-, lemon- or orange-
    flavoured yogurt ice**
icing (confectioners') sugar, for dusting

1 Remove the basil leaves from the stems and tear them into small pieces. Cut away the skin from the pineapple, then halve the fruit and remove the core. Chop the flesh into chunks. Push the pineapple through a juicer with the basil. Chill until ready to serve.

2 Pour the juice into 2 glasses and add two scoops of yogurt ice to each. Decorate with basil sprigs and dust lightly with icing sugar.

Nutritional information per portion: Energy 353kcal/1488kJ; Protein 5.7g; Carbohydrate 58.5g, of which sugars 57.3g; Fat 12.3g, of which saturates 7.2g; Cholesterol 11mg; Calcium 162mg; Fibre 3.6g; Sodium 99mg.

Iced mango lassi

Based on a traditional Indian drink, this will go down well served with spicy food at dinner, at long, hot garden parties, or as a welcome cooler at any time of day. In fact, it is perfect for just about any social occasion.

MAKES 3–4 GLASSES

175g/6oz/scant 1 cup caster (superfine)
    sugar
150ml/¼ pint/⅔ cup water
2 lemons
500ml/17fl oz/generous 2 cups Greek
    (US strained plain) yogurt
350ml/12fl oz/1½ cups mango juice
ice cubes (optional)
fresh mint sprigs and mango wedges,
    to decorate

1 Gently heat the sugar and water in a pan, stirring until the sugar dissolves. Pour into a jug (pitcher). Leave to cool, then chill until very cold.

2 Add the grated rind and juice of the lemons to the chilled syrup and stir well. Freeze in a shallow container until thickened. Beat in the yogurt and return to the freezer until thick enough to scoop.

3 To serve, blend the mango juice and 10 small scoops of yogurt ice in a blender/food processor until smooth. Top each drink with another scoop of the yogurt ice and decorate with mint sprigs and mango wedges.

Nutritional information per portion: Energy 366kcal/1546kJ; Protein 8.8g; Carbohydrate 60.6g, of which sugars 60.3g; Fat 12.9g, of which saturates 6.6g; Cholesterol 0mg; Calcium 221mg; Fibre 2.3g; Sodium 93mg.

White chocolate and hazelnut cream

This luxurious combination of smooth, creamy white chocolate and crunchy hazelnut is simply irresistible. To get the most flavour from the hazelnuts, it is always best to use whole ones, toasting them first to develop their nuttiness and then grinding them fresh.

MAKES 3 GLASSES

90g/3¹/₂oz/scant 1 cup blanched hazelnuts
150g/5oz white chocolate
300ml/¹/₂ pint/1¹/₄ cups full cream (whole) milk
4 large scoops white chocolate or vanilla ice cream
a little freshly grated nutmeg (optional)

1 Roughly chop the hazelnuts using a large, sharp knife, then toast them lightly in a dry frying pan, turning continuously to ensure that they are toasted evenly. Reserve 30ml/2 tbsp for decoration, then tip the remainder into a blender or food processor. Blend until very finely ground.

2 Finely chop the chocolate and reserve 30ml/2 tbsp for decoration. Put the remainder in a small, heavy pan with half of the milk and heat very gently until the chocolate has melted thoroughly. Stir until smooth, then pour the chocolate into a bowl. Add the remaining milk, stir and leave to cool.

3 Add the melted chocolate mixture to the blender with the ice cream and a little grated nutmeg, if using. Blend until smooth. Pour into glasses and sprinkle with the reserved hazelnuts and chocolate. Grate over a little extra nutmeg, if you like, and serve immediately.

Nutritional information per portion: Energy 703kcal/2927kJ; Protein 15.1g; Carbohydrate 55.3g, of which sugars 53.6g; Fat 47g, of which saturates 19.2g; Cholesterol 38mg; Calcium 395mg; Fibre 1.9g; Sodium 160mg.

Ice cool coconut

Instead of coconut milk, this recipe opts for desiccated coconut steeped in water, which is then strained to extract the flavour. Without the nutty texture, this delicious coconut feast slides down very nicely on a summer's evening. As a treat, add a splash of coconut liqueur.

MAKES 2–3 GLASSES

150g/5oz/2¹/₂ cups desiccated (dry unsweetened shredded) coconut
30ml/2 tbsp lime juice
30ml/2 tbsp icing (confectioners') sugar, plus extra for dusting
200g/7oz vanilla iced non-dairy dessert
lime slices, to decorate

1 Put the coconut in a heatproof bowl and add 600ml/1 pint/2¹/₂ cups boiling water. Leave to stand for 30 minutes. Strain the coconut through a sieve (strainer) lined with muslin (cheesecloth) into a bowl, pressing the pulp with a spoon to extract as much juice as possible. Discard the pulp and chill the coconut milk.

2 Pour the coconut milk into a blender or food processor with the lime juice, sugar and non-dairy dessert. Then blend thoroughly until completely smooth. Pour into glasses and decorate with lime slices. Lightly dust the lime slices and edges of the glasses with icing sugar and serve immediately.

Nutritional information per portion: Energy 443kcal/1841kJ; Protein 4.9g; Carbohydrate 26.2g, of which sugars 25.7g; Fat 36.2g, of which saturates 29.9g; Cholesterol 5mg; Calcium 65mg; Fibre 6.9g; Sodium 56mg.

Fire and ice

This unconventional frozen yogurt drink is flavoured with fresh orange juice and specks of hot red chilli. It's great on a hot summer's day, after lunch or any other time when you're in need of a refreshing boost. If you've plenty of time on your hands, add an alcoholic kick to the drink by drizzling each glass with a splash of orange liqueur before serving.

MAKES 2–3 TALL GLASSES

90g/3¹⁄₂oz/¹⁄₂ cup caster (superfine)
   sugar
1 lemon
300ml/¹⁄₂ pint/1¹⁄₄ cups freshly
   squeezed orange juice
200g/7oz/scant 1 cup Greek (US strained
   plain) yogurt
1 red chilli, seeded and finely chopped
60ml/4 tbsp Cointreau or other orange-
   flavoured liqueur (optional)
orange slices and extra chillies, to
   decorate

1 Put the sugar in a pan with 100ml/3¹⁄₂fl oz/scant ¹⁄₂ cup water and heat gently, stirring with a spoon until the sugar has dissolved. Pour into a freezer container and leave to cool. Finely grate the rind of the lemon and juice.

2 Add the lemon rind and juice and 100ml/3¹⁄₂fl oz/scant ¹⁄₂ cup of the orange juice. Freeze for 2 hours or until a band of ice has formed around the edges. Turn into a bowl and add the yogurt and chopped chilli. Whisk until thick. Freeze for 1–2 hours until almost solid.

3 To serve, scoop the frozen yogurt into a blender or food processor and add the remaining orange juice. Process until very thick and smooth. Pour into tall glasses and drizzle with a little liqueur, if using. Serve with straws and decorate with orange slices and fresh chillies.

Nutritional information per portion: Energy 234kcal/989kJ; Protein 5.4g; Carbohydrate 41.6g, of which sugars 41.6g; Fat 7g, of which saturates 3.5g; Cholesterol 0mg; Calcium 131mg; Fibre 0.1g; Sodium 60mg.

Cool as a currant

Tiny, glossy blackcurrants are a virtual powerhouse of nutrients, packed with vitamins C and E, as well as essential iron, calcium and magnesium. Whizzed in a blender with plenty of crushed ice, they make a drink so deliciously thick and slushy that you might want to serve it with long spoons so that you can scoop up every last drop.

MAKES 2 TALL GLASSES

125g/4¼oz/generous 1 cup
   blackcurrants, plus extra to decorate
60ml/4 tbsp light muscovado
   (brown) sugar
good pinch of mixed (apple pie) spice
   (optional)
225g/8oz/2 cups crushed ice

1 Put the blackcurrants and sugar in a pan. (There is no need to string the blackcurrants first.) Add the mixed spice, if using, and pour in 100ml/3½ fl oz/scant ½ cup water. Bring to the boil and cook for 2–3 minutes until the blackcurrants are completely soft.

2 Press the mixture through a sieve (strainer) into a bowl, pressing the pulp with the back of a wooden spoon to extract as much juice as possible. Leave to stand until it has completely cooled.

3 Put the crushed ice in a blender or food processor with the cooled juice and blend for about 1 minute until slushy. Pour into glasses, decorate with blackcurrants and serve immediately.

Nutritional information per portion: Energy 136kcal/580kJ; Protein 0.7g; Carbohydrate 35.5g, of which sugars 35.5g; Fat 0g, of which saturates 0g; Cholesterol 0mg; Calcium 54mg; Fibre 2.3g; Sodium 4mg.

Rum and raisin thick-shake

This rich and creamy milkshake, based on the classic combination of rum and raisins, is remarkably easy to prepare. Use a good quality ice cream, leave it to soften slightly in the refrigerator before scooping, and you simply can't go wrong.

MAKES 2 TALL GLASSES

75g/3oz/generous ½ cup raisins

45ml/3 tbsp dark rum

300ml/½ pint/1¼ cups full cream (whole) milk

500ml/17fl oz/2¼ cups good quality vanilla ice cream

1 Put the raisins, rum and a little of the milk into a blender or food processor and process for about 1 minute, or until the raisins are finely chopped.

2 Spoon two large scoops of the vanilla ice cream into two tall glasses and put the remaining ice cream and milk into the blender. Process until creamy.

3 Pour the milkshake into glasses and serve immediately with straws and long spoons for scooping up the raisins.

Nutritional information per portion: Energy 789kcal/3288kJ; Protein 15.5g; Carbohydrate 74.8g, of which sugars 74.5g; Fat 43.8g, of which saturates 26.4g; Cholesterol 21mg; Calcium 445mg; Fibre 0.8g; Sodium 237mg.

Espresso crush

This creatively layered treat combines slushy frozen granita with a thick vanilla ice cream layer, and is perfect for rounding off a lazy summer lunch or as a late afternoon refresher. The granita needs several hours in the freezer but will keep for weeks.

MAKES 4 GLASSES

75ml/5 tbsp ground espresso coffee
75g/3oz/scant ¹/₂ cup caster (superfine) sugar
300g/11oz vanilla ice cream or vanilla iced non-dairy dessert
75ml/5 tbsp milk or soya milk

1 Put the coffee in a cafetière, add 750ml/1¹/₄ pints/3 cups boiling water and leave for 5 minutes. Plunge the cafetière and pour the coffee into a shallow freezer container. Stir in the sugar until dissolved. Leave to cool completely, then cover and freeze until slushy around the edges.

2 Break up the ice crystals, stirring them into the centre of the container. Re-freeze until slushy around the edges again. Repeat forking and stirring until completely slushy with no liquid remaining. Re-freeze until ready to use.

3 Put the ice cream or iced dessert and milk in a blender and process until thick and smooth. To serve, spoon a little into the base of each glass and sprinkle with a layer of the granita. Repeat layering until the glasses are full.

Nutritional information per portion: Energy 217kcal/915kJ; Protein 3.4g; Carbohydrate 39g, of which sugars 38.3g; Fat 6.3g, of which saturates 4.1g; Cholesterol 21mg; Calcium 115mg; Fibre 0g; Sodium 55mg.

Tempting dessert drinks

Here, irresistible blends that imitate

popular desserts are cleverly transformed

into stunning drinks you can sip leisurely

or, in some cases, scoop with a spoon.

Be tempted by true classics such as

sparkling peach melba and blueberry

meringue crumble or, for something sweet

and tempting, try a cool chocolate float or

a twist on banoffee pie – banoffee high.

Sparkling peach melba

Serve this fresh and fruity drink during the summer months when raspberries and peaches are at their sweetest and best. Traditional cream soda gives this drink a really smooth flavour and a lovely fizz, while the optional shot of Drambuie or brandy gives it a definite kick.

MAKES 2 GLASSES

300g/11oz/scant 2 cups raspberries
2 large ripe peaches
30ml/2 tbsp Drambuie or brandy
    (optional)
15ml/1 tbsp icing (confectioners') sugar
cream soda, to serve

1 Pack a few raspberries into six tiny shot glasses, or into six sections of an ice cube tray, and pour over water to cover. Freeze for several hours.

2 Halve and stone the peaches and cut one half into thin slices. Reserve 115g/4oz/²/₃ cup of the raspberries. Divide the rest, and the peach slices, between two tall stemmed glasses. Drizzle with the liqueur, if using.

3 Push the reserved raspberries and the remaining peach flesh through the juicer. Stir the icing sugar into the juice and pour the juice over the fruits.

4 Turn the raspberry-filled ice cubes out of the shot glasses or ice cube tray and add three to each glass. Top up with cream soda and serve immediately.

Nutritional information per portion: Energy 100kcal/432kJ; Protein 3.2g; Carbohydrate 22.4g, of which sugars 22.4g; Fat 0.6g, of which saturates 0.2g; Cholesterol 0mg; Calcium 49mg; Fibre 5.3g; Sodium 6mg.

Black beauty

This is the classic partnership of apples and tart blackberries. The sweetness of the apples is balanced deliciously by the sharp tang and vibrant colour of the ripe berries. If you cannot find fresh blackberries, use other deep red fruits such as mulberries or loganberries.

MAKES 2–3 TALL GLASSES

30ml/2 tbsp golden caster
   (superfine) sugar
2.5ml/1/2 tsp ground cinnamon
3 eating apples
200g/7oz/13/4 cups blackberries
ice cubes
borage, to decorate (optional)

1 Put the sugar in a small bowl. Add the cinnamon and 60ml/4 tbsp boiling water and stir until the sugar dissolves to form a syrup.

2 Roughly chop the apples. Push the blackberries through a juicer and follow with the apples. Pour in the sugar syrup and stir well to mix.

3 Pour the juice into tall glasses and add several ice cubes to each one. Decorate the drinks with sprigs of borage or individual borage flowers, if using, and serve immediately.

Nutritional information per portion: Energy 91kcal/388kJ; Protein 1g; Carbohydrate 22.8g, of which sugars 22.8g; Fat 0.2g, of which saturates 0g; Cholesterol 0mg; Calcium 37mg; Fibre 3.7g; Sodium 4mg.

Banoffee high

Make plenty of this outrageous, lip-smacking milkshake because everyone will love it. Nobody is pretending this is a health drink, but it is guaranteed to give you an energy rush of astronomic proportions. Keep any leftover syrup in the refrigerator to use as a quick and delicious toffee sauce for spooning over ice cream.

MAKES 4 TALL GLASSES

75g/3oz/scant ¹/₂ cup light muscovado (brown) sugar
150ml/¹/₄ pint/²/₃ cup double (heavy) cream
4 large bananas

600ml/1 pint/2¹/₂ cups full cream (whole) milk
15ml/1 tbsp vanilla sugar
8 ice cubes

1 To make the toffee syrup, put the sugar in a small heavy pan with 75ml/ 5 tbsp water. Heat gently, stirring until the sugar dissolves, then add 45ml/ 3 tbsp of the cream and bring to the boil. Let the syrup simmer for about 4 minutes until thickened. Remove from the heat and leave to cool for about 30 minutes.

2 Peel the bananas, break into pieces and put into a blender or food processor with the milk, vanilla sugar, ice cubes and a further 45ml/3 tbsp of the cream. Blend until smooth and frothy.

3 Pour the remaining cream into a bowl and whip lightly with a whisk or hand-held electric mixer until it just holds its shape.

4 Add half the toffee syrup to the milkshake and blend, then pour into glasses. Drizzle more syrup around the insides of the glasses. Spoon the whipped cream over and drizzle with any remaining syrup. Serve immediately.

Nutritional information per portion: Energy 469kcal/1958kJ; Protein 6.9g; Carbohydrate 54.1g, of which sugars 51.8g; Fat 26.3g, of which saturates 16.4g; Cholesterol 72mg; Calcium 213mg; Fibre 1.1g; Sodium 75mg.

Super sorbet fizz

Freshly blended pineapple and cool, tangy lemon sorbet, topped up with sparkling ginger ale, make a tastebud-tingling, fantastically mouthwatering drink. This semi-frozen blend is perfect after a summer lunch as a light alternative to more conventional desserts.

MAKES 4 GLASSES

30ml/2 tbsp muscovado (molasses) sugar

15ml/1 tbsp lemon juice

½ pineapple

1 piece preserved stem ginger, roughly chopped

200ml/7fl oz/scant 1 cup lemon sorbet, slightly softened

wafer thin pineapple and lemon slices, to decorate

ginger ale, to serve

1 Mix the sugar with the lemon juice in a small bowl and leave to stand for about 5 minutes until it turns syrupy.

2 Discard the skin and core from the pineapple and cut the flesh into chunks. Put the chunks in a blender or food processor with the ginger and whizz until smooth, scraping down the side of the bowl once or twice, if necessary.

3 Add the sorbet and process briefly until smooth. Spoon the muscovado syrup into four tumblers, then pour in the pineapple mixture.

4 Decorate the edge of the glasses with the pineapple and lemon slices. Top up each glass with ginger ale and serve immediately.

Nutritional information per portion: Energy 126kcal/539kJ; Protein 0.8g; Carbohydrate 32.5g, of which sugars 32.5g; Fat 0.2g, of which saturates 0g; Cholesterol 0mg; Calcium 19mg; Fibre 0.9g; Sodium 11mg.

Blueberry meringue crumble

This drink combines fresh tangy fruit, crisp sugary meringue and plenty of vanilla-scented cream in one delicious milkshake. Iced yogurt is used to provide a slightly lighter note than ice cream, but there's nothing to stop you using ice cream instead for an even greater indulgence.

MAKES 3–4 TALL GLASSES

150g/5oz/1¼ cups fresh blueberries, plus extra to decorate

15ml/1 tbsp icing (confectioners') sugar

250ml/8fl oz/1 cup vanilla iced yogurt

200ml/7fl oz/scant 1 cup full cream (whole) milk

30ml/2 tbsp lime juice

75g/3oz meringues, lightly crushed

1 Put the blueberries and sugar in a blender or food processor with 60ml/ 4 tbsp water and blend until smooth. Transfer the purée to a small bowl and rinse out the blender.

2 Process the iced yogurt, milk and lime juice in the blender until thoroughly combined. Add half of the crushed meringues and process until smooth.

3 Pour alternate layers of the milkshake, blueberry syrup and the remaining crushed meringues into tall glasses, finishing with a few chunks of meringue.

4 Drizzle any remaining blueberry syrup over the tops of the meringues and decorate with a few extra blueberries. Serve immediately.

Nutritional information per portion: Energy 254kcal/1072kJ; Protein 5.6g; Carbohydrate 45.1g, of which sugars 41.5g; Fat 6.9g, of which saturates 3.8g; Cholesterol 11mg; Calcium 151mg; Fibre 0.8g; Sodium 80mg.

Coconut and passion fruit ice

Few things beat the unadulterated, pure flavour of freshly juiced coconut. Whizzed with plenty of crushed ice and teamed with sharp, intensely flavoured passion fruit, it produces a milkshake that tastes indulgently good but is still refreshingly natural and wholesome.

MAKES 2–3 TALL GLASSES

1 coconut
75ml/5 tbsp icing (confectioners') sugar
3 passion fruit
150g/5oz crushed ice
60ml/4 tbsp double (heavy) cream

1 Drain the milk from the coconut and put to one side. Break open the coconut, remove the flesh, then pare off the brown skin. Push the coconut pieces through a juicer along with 150ml/$^1/_4$ pint/$^2/_3$ cup water. Stir the icing sugar into the juice and reserve.

2 Halve the passion fruit and scoop the pulp into a small bowl. Set aside.

3 Put the crushed ice in a blender or food processor and blend until slushy. Add the juiced coconut, any drained coconut milk and the cream. Process enough to just blend the ingredients.

4 Pour the mixture into tall stemmed glasses, then, using a teaspoon, spoon the passion fruit on top of the drink. Add stirrers, if you like, and serve.

Nutritional information per portion: Energy 247kcal/1041kJ; Protein 1.4g; Carbohydrate 37.1g, of which sugars 37.1g; Fat 11.4g, of which saturates 7.1g; Cholesterol 27mg; Calcium 83mg; Fibre 0.5g; Sodium 75mg.

Death by chocolate

There are only two ingredients used in this decadently rich smoothie: creamy milk and the best chocolate that money can buy. Blended together, they make the frothiest, smoothest and most deliciously chocolatey drink you will ever taste.

MAKES 2 LARGE GLASSES

150g/5oz good quality chocolate
350ml/12fl oz/1$^1/_2$ cups full cream (whole) milk
ice cubes
chocolate curls or shavings, to serve

1 Break the chocolate into pieces and place in a heatproof bowl set over a pan of simmering water, making sure that the bowl does not rest in the water.

2 Add 60ml/4 tbsp of the milk and then leave until the chocolate melts, stirring occasionally with a wooden spoon.

3 Remove the bowl from the heat, pour the remaining milk over the chocolate and stir to combine.

4 Pour the mixture into a blender or food processor and blend until frothy. Pour into glasses, add ice and chocolate curls or shavings, then serve.

Nutritional information per portion: Energy 463kcal/1944kJ; Protein 9.7g; Carbohydrate 55.9g, of which sugars 55.2g; Fat 24g, of which saturates 14.5g; Cholesterol 15mg; Calcium 235mg; Fibre 1.9g; Sodium 80mg.

Turkish delight

If you like Turkish delight, you'll love this fabulously indulgent drink. With the scented aroma of rose water and the delicious icy sweetness of vanilla ice cream, it is difficult to imagine a more decadent, or delicious, combination of ingredients.

MAKES 3–4 GLASSES

125g/4¼oz rose-flavoured Turkish delight

475ml/16fl oz/2 cups semi-skimmed (low-fat) milk

250ml/8fl oz/1 cup good quality vanilla ice cream

a little finely grated plain (semisweet) chocolate, or drinking chocolate powder, for sprinkling (optional)

1 Roughly chop the Turkish delight and reserve a few pieces for decoration. Put the rest in a pan with half the milk. Heat gently until the pieces begin to melt. Remove the pan from the heat and leave to cool.

2 Spoon the mixture into a blender or food processor and add the remaining milk. Process until smooth, then add the ice cream and blend briefly to combine. Pour into glasses, top with the reserved Turkish delight and serve, sprinkled with chocolate or drinking chocolate, if using.

Nutritional information per portion: Energy 258kcal/1088kJ; Protein 6.5g; Carbohydrate 42.3g, of which sugars 38.7g; Fat 7.4g, of which saturates 5.1g; Cholesterol 22mg; Calcium 208mg; Fibre 0g; Sodium 98mg.

Nutty nougat

For the best results, chill this glorious milkshake for a few hours until it is icy cold and the ingredients have had time to fuse into a hedonistic delight. Skinning the pistachio nuts is not essential, but it transforms them from dull green to a gorgeous, vivid emerald colour.

MAKES 3 GLASSES

90ml/6 tbsp sweetened condensed milk

300ml/¹/₂ pint/1¹/₄ cups semi-skimmed (low-fat) milk

100ml/3¹/₂ fl oz/scant ¹/₂ cup crème fraîche

15ml/1 tbsp lemon juice

25g/1oz/¹/₄ cup skinned pistachio nuts

25g/1oz/¹/₄ cup blanched almonds

25g/1oz/3 tbsp candied peel, finely chopped, plus extra for decoration

ice cubes

1 Put the condensed milk and the semi-skimmed milk in a blender or food processor. Add the crème fraîche and blend until combined.

2 Add the lemon juice, pistachio nuts, almonds and chopped peel to the blender or food processor and blend until chopped into tiny pieces. Pour over ice cubes in glasses, add a few slices of candied peel and serve.

Nutritional information per portion: Energy 392kcal/1636kJ; Protein 10g; Carbohydrate 28.3g, of which sugars 27.8g; Fat 27.4g, of which saturates 13g; Cholesterol 54mg; Calcium 266mg; Fibre 1.5g; Sodium 161mg.

Coffee frappé

This creamy, smooth creation (strictly for adults because of the alcoholic content) makes a wonderful alternative to a dessert. Serve in small glasses or little cappuccino cups for a glamorous touch, and provide your guests with both straws and long-handled spoons.

MAKES 4 GLASSES

8 scoops of classic coffee ice cream
90ml/6 tbsp Kahlúa or Tia Maria liqueur
150ml/¼ pint/⅔ cup single (light) cream
1.5ml/¼ tsp ground cinnamon (optional)
crushed ice
ground cinnamon, for sprinkling

1 Put half the coffee ice cream in a food processor or blender. Add the liqueur, then pour in the cream with a little cinnamon, if using, and blend. Scoop the remaining ice cream into four glasses or cappuccino cups.

2 Using a dessertspoon, spoon the coffee cream over the ice cream in each glass, then top with a little crushed ice. Sprinkle the top of each frappé with a little ground cinnamon and serve immediately.

COOK'S TIP
To make a non-alcoholic version of this drink, simply substitute strong black coffee for the Kahlúa or Tia Maria.

Nutritional information per portion: Energy 489kcal/2049kJ; Protein 8.3g; Carbohydrate 57.6g, of which sugars 55.6g; Fat 23.2g, of which saturates 15g; Cholesterol 73mg; Calcium 255mg; Fibre 0g; Sodium 136mg.

Cool chocolate float

Frothy, chocolatey milkshake and scoops of creamy sweet chocolate and vanilla ice cream combine to make the most meltingly delicious drink ever. For lovers of ice cream and chocolate, whether adults or children, this one is sure to be a triumph.

MAKES 2 TALL GLASSES

115g/4oz plain (semisweet) chocolate, broken into pieces
250ml/8fl oz/1 cup milk
15ml/1 tbsp caster (superfine) sugar
4 large scoops of classic vanilla ice cream
4 large scoops of dark (bittersweet) chocolate ice cream
a little lightly whipped cream
grated chocolate or chocolate curls, to decorate

1 Put the chocolate in a heavy pan and add the milk and sugar. Heat gently, stirring with a wooden spoon until the chocolate has melted and the mixture is smooth. Leave to cool.

2 Blend the cooled chocolate mixture with half of the ice cream in a blender or food processor.

3 Scoop the remaining ice cream alternately into two tall glasses: vanilla then chocolate. Using a dessertspoon, drizzle the chocolate milk over and around the ice cream in each glass. Top with lightly whipped cream and sprinkle over a little grated chocolate or some chocolate curls to decorate. Serve immediately.

Nutritional information per portion: Energy 918kcal/3834kJ; Protein 16.9g; Carbohydrate 92.3g, of which sugars 91.5g; Fat 56g, of which saturates 33.7g; Cholesterol 11mg; Calcium 423mg; Fibre 1.5g; Sodium 208mg.

Party drinks

If you're entertaining a large crowd, whizzing up a choice of interesting party brews is a sure-fire way to get the occasion off to a lively start. From long and refreshing spritzers to short, punchy tipples, this chapter offers a feast of innovative choices that include a couple of fresh fruit blends for partygoers who prefer not to drink alcohol.

Frozen margarita

For the serious cocktail connoisseur, a margarita sipped with a slice of lime from the salt-crusted rim of a glass is simply the best choice. A classic citrus juicer will help you to get the maximum juice from limes, but if the fruits are very firm and don't yield much juice, you could try giving them a brief blast in the microwave first.

MAKES 8 SMALL GLASSES

150ml/¼ pint/⅔ cup lime juice, from about 6 large limes
sea salt flakes
120ml/4fl oz/½ cup Cointreau or Grand Marnier

200ml/7fl oz/scant 1 cup tequila
150g/5oz crushed ice
1 lime, thinly sliced, to decorate

1 To coat the glass rims with salt, put 30ml/2 tbsp of the lime juice into a saucer and plenty of salt flakes in another. Turn the glasses upside down and dip the rim of each glass in the lime juice, then in the salt. Invert the glasses again and put to one side.

2 Put the remaining lime juice in a blender or food processor with the Cointreau or Grand Marnier, tequila and ice. Process until the mixture is slushy.

3 Pour the margarita mixture into the salt-rimmed glasses, add a slice of lime to each glass and serve immediately.

COOK'S TIP
Gold tequila has aged in casks for longer than white and has a slightly golden tinge to it. Try to use clear tequila for this recipe as it will result in a fresh, clear cocktail in which the colour of the lime really shows through.

Nutritional information per portion: Energy 368kcal/1522kJ; Protein 0.1g; Carbohydrate 0.3g, of which sugars 0.3g; Fat 0g, of which saturates 0g; Cholesterol 0mg; Calcium 1mg; Fibre 0g; Sodium 0mg.

Tropical fruit royale

This fresh and fruity variation of a kir royale – in which Champagne is poured over crème de cassis – is made with tropical fruits and sparkling wine. A lot less expensive, it still has a wonderfully elegant feel. Blend the fruits ahead of time to give the mango ice cubes time to freeze.

MAKES 6 GLASSES

2 large mangoes
6 passion fruits
sparkling wine

1 Peel the mangoes, cut the flesh off the stone (pit), then put the flesh in a blender or food processor. Process until smooth, scraping the mixture down from the side of the bowl, if necessary.

2 Fill an ice-cube tray with half of the purée and freeze for 2 hours.

3 Cut six wedges from one or two of the passion fruits and scoop the pulp from the rest of the passion fruit into the remaining mango purée. Process until well blended.

4 Spoon the mixture into six stemmed glasses. Divide the mango ice cubes among the glasses, top up with sparkling wine and add the passion fruit wedges. Serve with stirrers, if you like.

Nutritional information per portion: Energy 136kcal/570kJ; Protein 1.2g; Carbohydrate 16.7g, of which sugars 16.5g; Fat 0.2g, of which saturates 0.1g; Cholesterol 0mg; Calcium 21mg; Fibre 2.2g; Sodium 11mg.

Pineapple and coconut rum crush

This thick and slushy tropical cooler is unbelievably rich thanks to the combination of coconut milk and thick cream. The addition of sweet, juicy, slightly tart pineapple, and finely crushed ice, offers a refreshing foil, making it all too easy to sip your way through several glasses.

MAKES 4–5 LARGE GLASSES

1 pineapple
30ml/2 tbsp lemon juice
200ml/7fl oz/scant 1 cup coconut milk
150ml/¼ pint/⅔ cup double (heavy) cream
200ml/7fl oz/scant 1 cup white rum
30–60ml/2–4 tbsp caster (superfine) sugar
500g/1¼lb finely crushed ice

1 Trim off the ends from the pineapple, then cut off the skin. Cut away the core and chop the flesh. Put the chopped flesh in a blender or food processor with the lemon juice and whizz until very smooth.

2 Add the coconut milk, cream, rum and 30ml/2 tbsp of the sugar. Blend until thoroughly combined, then taste and add more sugar if necessary. Pack the ice into glasses and pour the drink over. Serve immediately.

COOK'S TIP

This is a great cocktail for making ahead of time. Blend it in advance and chill in a jug (pitcher). Store the crushed ice in the freezer ready for serving as soon as it's required.

Nutritional information per portion: Energy 336kcal/1400kJ; Protein 1.3g; Carbohydrate 24.9g, of which sugars 24.9g; Fat 16.5g, of which saturates 10.1g; Cholesterol 41mg; Calcium 58mg; Fibre 1.9g; Sodium 54mg.

Raspberry rendezvous

Pink, raspberry-flavoured bubbles and a hint of brandy make this the ultimate in sippable sophistication. A splash of sweet, sugary grenadine added to the jewel-coloured raspberry juice smoothes out any hint of a sharp tang from slightly underripe fruit.

MAKES 6 TALL GLASSES

400g/14oz/2¹/₃ cups raspberries, plus extra raspberries, to serve
100ml/3¹/₂fl oz/scant ¹/₂ cup grenadine
100ml/3¹/₂fl oz/scant ¹/₂ cup brandy or cherry brandy
ice cubes
1 litre/1³/₄ pints/4 cups ginger ale

1 Push handfuls of the raspberries through a juicer and transfer the juice into a jug (pitcher).

2 Stir the grenadine and brandy or cherry brandy into the raspberry juice and chill (preferably overnight, but for at least 1 or 2 hours) until you are ready to serve it.

3 Prepare six tall glasses: add plenty of ice cubes to each and place a few extra raspberries in the bottom of the glasses.

4 Pour the raspberry mixture into each of the prepared glasses and then top up with the ginger ale. Serve the cocktails immediately.

Nutritional information per portion: Energy 122kcal/512kJ; Protein 0.9g; Carbohydrate 15g, of which sugars 15g; Fat 0.2g, of which saturates 0.1g; Cholesterol 0mg; Calcium 18mg; Fibre 1.7g; Sodium 4mg.

Scent sensation

Orange flower water, distilled from the delicate white blooms of the orange blossom tree, gives delicious sweet pear and redcurrant juices a delicate fragrance and the most subtle of flavours. Like rose water, it is often associated with Middle Eastern cooking.

MAKES 4–5 GLASSES

4 pears
300g/11oz/2³/₄ cups redcurrants
2 cinnamon sticks
45ml/3 tbsp orange flower water
about 25g/1oz/¹/₄ cup icing (confectioners') sugar
tonic water
cinnamon sticks and extra redcurrants, to decorate (optional)

1 Using a small, sharp knife, cut the pears into chunks of roughly the same size and push the chunks through a juicer with the redcurrants.

2 Crumble the two cinnamon sticks, using your fingers, and add to the redcurrant juice. Cover and leave to stand for at least 1 hour.

3 Strain the juice through a sieve (strainer) into a bowl, and then whisk in the orange flower water and a little icing sugar to taste.

4 To serve, put one or two cinnamon sticks in each glass, if using. Pour the juice into glasses, then top up with tonic water and decorate with the extra redcurrants, if you like.

Nutritional information per portion: Energy 85kcal/359kJ; Protein 0.9g; Carbohydrate 21.2g, of which sugars 21.2g; Fat 0.1g, of which saturates 0g; Cholesterol 0mg; Calcium 52mg; Fibre 4.8g; Sodium 6mg.

Watermelon gin

The fabulously red, juicy flesh of the watermelon makes a perfect partner for the strong, heady scent and flavour of gin. The juice is so sweet and delicate, and this sparkling drink is so stunningly pretty, that you'll be hard-pressed to resist its appeal. For a party, just make up a large jug of the juice, top up with tonic water and pour out for guests as they arrive.

MAKES 4 LARGE GLASSES

500g/1¼lb wedge watermelon
juice of 1 lime
10ml/2 tsp caster (superfine) sugar
crushed ice
150ml/¼ pint/⅔ cup gin
lime slices
tonic water

1 Cut off the skin from the watermelon and chop the flesh into large chunks, removing the seeds. Push the flesh through the juicer and pour into a large jug (pitcher). Stir in the lime juice and sugar and chill.

2 Half-fill glasses with crushed ice. Stir the gin into the juice and pour over the ice. Add the lime slices and top up with tonic water. Serve immediately.

COOK'S TIP
This recipe makes a cocktail that is not too alcoholic. For a slightly stronger drink, add up to 75ml/2½fl oz/⅓ cup more gin to the mix before you pour it over the ice.

Nutritional information per portion: Energy 132kcal/553kJ; Protein 0.6g; Carbohydrate 11.5g, of which sugars 11.5g; Fat 0.4g, of which saturates 0.1g; Cholesterol 0mg; Calcium 10mg; Fibre 0.1g; Sodium 3mg.

Blackcurrant cassis

Cassis is an intensely flavoured blackcurrant liqueur, and is generally used to add just a hint of colour and flavour to Champagne and sparkling wines. This home-made variation is so packed with the summer freshness of juicy blackcurrants, you'll want to ensure that it is the predominant flavour in any cocktail.

MAKES 6–8 GLASSES

225g/8oz/2 cups blackcurrants
50g/2oz/¼ cup caster (superfine) sugar
75ml/5 tbsp vodka
sparkling wine or Champagne

1 Strip the blackcurrants from their stems and scatter 50g/2oz/½ cup of the fruit into an ice-cube tray. Top up with cold water and freeze for 2 hours.

2 Put the sugar in a small, heavy pan with 60ml/4 tbsp water and heat gently until the sugar has dissolved. Bring to the boil, then pour into a jug (pitcher) and leave to cool. Push the remaining blackcurrants through a juicer and mix with the syrup. Stir in the vodka and chill until ready to serve.

3 Put two or three of the blackcurrant ice cubes into each tall-stemmed glass. Add 15–30ml/1–2 tbsp of the syrup to each glass and top up with sparkling wine or Champagne. Serve immediately.

Nutritional information per portion: Energy 53kcal/225kJ; Protein 0.3g; Carbohydrate 8.4g, of which sugars 8.4g; Fat 0g, of which saturates 0g; Cholesterol 0mg; Calcium 20mg; Fibre 1g; Sodium 1mg.

Mint julep

A julep is a sweetened, iced drink made using brandy or whisky and fresh mint leaves. This stunning version infuses the mint in sugar syrup to colour it a cooling shade of green. Pep up with brandy, or delicious peach brandy, and pour over ice for a summertime tipple.

MAKES 4 SMALL GLASSES

25g/1oz/2 tbsp caster (superfine) sugar
25g/1oz fresh mint, plus extra mint sprigs, to decorate
crushed ice
100ml/7 tbsp brandy or peach brandy

1 Put the sugar in a small, heavy pan with 200ml/ 7fl oz/scant 1 cup water. Heat gently until the sugar dissolves, then bring to the boil and boil for 1 minute to make a syrup. Pour into a small bowl. Pull the mint leaves from the stalks and add to the hot syrup. Leave the syrup to stand for about 30 minutes or until cool.

2 Strain the syrup into a blender or food processor, add the mint and blend lightly until it is finely chopped.

3 Half-fill four small glasses with crushed ice and put one or two mint sprigs into each glass. Then mix the brandy with the mint syrup and pour over the ice. Serve immediately.

Nutritional information per portion: Energy 83kcal/346kJ; Protein 0.3g; Carbohydrate 6.9g, of which sugars 6.5g; Fat 0.1g, of which saturates 0g; Cholesterol 0mg; Calcium 17mg; Fibre 0g; Sodium 1mg.

Lime mojito

Cuba and the Caribbean islands have invented some of the most delicious lime- and rum-based cocktails, from tangy, refreshing shorts to thick, creamy concoctions. This recipe fits the first category, but beware – you're bound to find it completely moreish.

MAKES 4 GLASSES

4 lemon balm sprigs
40ml/8 tsp caster (superfine) sugar
4 limes
130ml/4$\frac{1}{2}$fl oz/generous $\frac{1}{2}$ cup white rum
ice cubes
strips of pared lime rind, to decorate
sparkling mineral water, to serve

1 Pull the lemon balm leaves from their stems. Put 10ml/2 tsp of the sugar into each small glass.

2 Add several lemon balm leaves to each glass and lightly rub the leaves into the sugar, using the back of a teaspoon, to release their fragrance.

3 Squeeze the limes using a citrus juicer, or by hand, and then pour the juice into the glasses with the rum.

4 Add plenty of ice to each glass and decorate with pared lime rind. Serve immediately, topped up with sparkling mineral water.

Nutritional information per portion: Energy 112kcal/467kJ; Protein 0.1g; Carbohydrate 10.5g, of which sugars 10.5g; Fat 0g, of which saturates 0g; Cholesterol 0mg; Calcium 5mg; Fibre 0g; Sodium 1mg.

Foaming citrus eggnog

For most of us, eggnog is inextricably associated with the festive season. This version, however, pepped up with orange rind and juice for a lighter, fresher taste, has a much wider appeal. Whether you sip it as a late-night soother, serve it as a wintry dessert or enjoy it as a cosy tipple on a wet afternoon, it's sure to bring a warm, rosy glow to your cheeks.

MAKES 2 GLASSES

2 small oranges
150ml/¼ pint/⅔ cup single (light)
  cream
plenty of freshly grated nutmeg
2.5ml/½ tsp ground cinnamon
2.5ml/½ tsp cornflour (cornstarch)
2 eggs, separated
30ml/2 tbsp light muscovado (brown)
  sugar
45ml/3 tbsp brandy
extra nutmeg, for sprinkling (optional)

1 Finely grate the rind from the oranges, then squeeze out the juice and pour it into a jug (pitcher).

2 Gently heat the rind in a small heavy pan with the cream, nutmeg, cinnamon and cornflour, stirring frequently until bubbling.

3 Whisk the egg yolks with the sugar, using a handheld whisk. Stir the hot citrus cream mixture into the egg yolks, then return to the pan. Pour in the orange juice and brandy and heat very gently, stirring until slightly thickened.

4 Whisk the egg whites in a large, clean bowl until foamy and light.

5 Strain the cream mixture through a sieve (strainer) into the whisked whites. Stir gently and pour into heatproof punch cups, handled glasses or mugs. Sprinkle over a little extra nutmeg before serving.

Nutritional information per portion: Energy 375kcal/1566kJ; Protein 9.1g; Carbohydrate 29.6g, of which sugars 29.6g; Fat 19.9g, of which saturates 10.7g; Cholesterol 232mg; Calcium 112mg; Fibre 0.1g; Sodium 98mg.

Amaretto apricot dream

This really is a dream of a drink, combining fresh, ripe apricots, oranges and delicious maple syrup with creamy cool yogurt. Light and fruity, it is a wonderful choice for a breezy, sunny day in the garden, and the addition of almond liqueur and amaretti biscuits gives it a wonderfully complex flavour. Once you've tasted one, you'll surely be back for more.

MAKES 4 GLASSES

3 large oranges
600g/1lb 6oz small fresh apricots
60ml/4 tbsp maple syrup, plus extra
   to serve
50g/2oz amaretti
200g/7oz/scant 1 cup Greek (US strained
   plain) yogurt
30ml/2 tbsp amaretto liqueur
mineral water (optional)
ice cubes

1 Grate the rind from one of the oranges and squeeze the juice from all three. Halve and stone (pit) the apricots and put them in a pan.

2 Add the orange juice and zest, cover with a lid and simmer very gently for 3 minutes or until the apricots are tender. Strain through a sieve (strainer), keeping the juice. Cool.

3 Put half the fruit, the strained juice, maple syrup and amaretti in a food processor or blender and

blend until completely smooth. Then, arrange the remaining fruit halves in the bases of four drinking glasses.

4 Stir the yogurt until smooth and then spoon half over the fruits. Add the amaretto, and a little mineral water to the mixture (if the juice is too thick), and pour into the glasses. Add the remaining yogurt and one or two ice cubes to each glass. Drizzle with maple syrup to serve.

Nutritional information per portion: Energy 397kcal/1690kJ; Protein 9.5g; Carbohydrate 86g, of which sugars 80.6g; Fat 3.1g, of which saturates 1g; Cholesterol 1mg; Calcium 227mg; Fibre 9.7g; Sodium 149mg.

Lemon vodka

Very similar to the deliciously moreish Italian liqueur, Limoncello, this lemon vodka should be drunk in small quantities due to its hefty alcoholic punch. Blend the sugar, lemons and vodka and keep in a bottle in the refrigerator, ready for pouring over crushed ice or topping up with soda or sparkling water. It is also delicious drizzled over melting vanilla ice cream.

MAKES 12–15 SMALL GLASSES

10 large lemons
275g/10oz/generous 1¼ cups caster (superfine) sugar
250ml/8fl oz/1 cup vodka
ice cubes

1 Squeeze the lemons using a citrus juicer. Pour the juice into a jug (pitcher), add the sugar and whisk well until all the sugar has dissolved.

2 Strain the sweetened lemon juice into a clean bottle or narrow-necked jar and add the vodka. Shake the mixture well to combine, and chill for up to 2 weeks.

3 To serve, fill small glasses with ice and pour the lemon vodka over.

Nutritional information per portion: Energy 126kcal/533kJ; Protein 0.2g; Carbohydrate 19.7g, of which sugars 19.7g; Fat 0g, of which saturates 0g; Cholesterol 0mg; Calcium 12mg; Fibre 0g; Sodium 1mg.

Apple-tice

Even the dullest of eating apples seem to juice well. With the addition of a fresh mint syrup and sparkling cider, any apple juice can be transformed into a distinctly exciting, mildly alcoholic blend that makes an excellent party drink. The recipe allows you to choose how much cider you add to each glass, which makes it easier to control your alcohol consumption.

MAKES 6–8 GLASSES

25g/1oz/1 cup mint leaves, plus extra
    mint sprigs, to decorate
15g/¹/₂oz/1 tbsp caster (superfine)
    sugar
6 eating apples
ice cubes
1 litre/1³/₄ pints/4 cups dry (hard) cider

1 Using scissors, roughly snip the mint into a heatproof jug (pitcher). Add the sugar to the jug, then pour over 200ml/7fl oz/scant 1 cup of boiling water. Stir well until the sugar has dissolved, then leave to stand until cool.

2 Drain the mint from the syrup and discard the mint leaves. Core the apples, chop them into equal-size chunks and push them through a juicer.

3 Mix the apple juice and mint-flavoured syrup in a large jug and chill (preferably overnight, but for at least 1–2 hours) until ready to serve.

4 To serve, add ice cubes and mint sprigs and top up with cider.

Nutritional information per portion: Energy 76kcal/322kJ; Protein 0.3g; Carbohydrate 10.9g, of which sugars 10.8g; Fat 0.1g, of which saturates 0g; Cholesterol 0mg; Calcium 20mg; Fibre 1g; Sodium 11mg.

Cranberry and apple spritzer

Don't leave the non-drinkers at your party with just the mixers, fizzy drinks or tap water. They'll love this cool, colourful spritzer, which combines tangy cranberries with fresh, juicy apples and a subtle, fragrant hint of vanilla, topped up with sparkling mineral water.

MAKES 6–8 GLASSES

6 red eating apples
375g/13oz/3½ cups fresh or frozen cranberries,
    plus extra to decorate
45ml/3 tbsp vanilla syrup
ice cubes
sparkling mineral water

1 Quarter and core the apples, then cut the flesh into pieces small enough to fit through a juicer. Push the cranberries and apple chunks through the juicer. Add the vanilla syrup to the juice and chill until ready to serve.

2 Pour the juice into glasses and add one or two ice cubes to each. Top up with sparkling mineral water and decorate with extra cranberries, threaded on to cocktail sticks (toothpicks). Serve immediately.

COOK'S TIP
To make vanilla syrup, heat a vanilla pod (bean) with sugar and water in a pan until the sugar dissolves. Simmer for 5 minutes, then leave to cool.

Nutritional information per portion: Energy 59kcal/255kJ; Protein 0.4g; Carbohydrate 15.3g, of which sugars 15.3g; Fat 0.1g, of which saturates 0g; Cholesterol 0mg; Calcium 6mg; Fibre 2g; Sodium 18mg.

Raspberry and grapefruit perfection

Make plenty of freshly juiced blends like this gorgeous combination and your guests will keep coming back for more. Raspberry and grapefruit juice make a great partnership, particularly if you add a little cinnamon syrup to counteract any tartness in the fruit.

MAKES 8 TALL GLASSES

1 cinnamon stick
50g/2oz/¼ cup caster (superfine) sugar
4 pink grapefruits
250g/9oz/1½ cups fresh or frozen raspberries
wedge of watermelon
crushed ice
borage flowers, to decorate (optional)

1 Gently heat the cinnamon stick in a small pan with the sugar and 200ml/7fl oz/scant 1 cup water until the sugar has dissolved, then bring to the boil and boil for 1 minute. Reserve to cool.

2 Cut away the skins from the pink grapefruits. Cut the flesh into small pieces for juicing. Juice the grapefruits and raspberries and pour into a small glass jug (pitcher).

3 Remove the cinnamon from the syrup and add the syrup to the grapefruit and raspberry juice in the jug.

4 Slice the watermelon into long thin wedges and place in eight tall glasses. Half-fill with crushed ice and sprinkle with borage flowers. Pour over the fruit juice and serve immediately.

Nutritional information per portion: Energy 64kcal/273kJ; Protein 1.2g; Carbohydrate 15.2g, of which sugars 15.2g; Fat 0.3g, of which saturates 0.1g; Cholesterol 0mg; Calcium 31mg; Fibre 1.9g; Sodium 4mg.

Happy days

Set a midsummer drinks party off to a good start with this fabulously fruity blend. It's packed with summer fruits and flavoured with refreshingly light, but highly intoxicating, Limoncello – a welcome alternative to the more traditional spirits used in party blends.

MAKES 8 GLASSES

250g/9oz/generous 2 cups redcurrants

675g/1¹/₂lb/6 cups strawberries

200ml/7fl oz/scant 1 cup Limoncello liqueur

ice cubes

small handful of mint or lemon balm

l litre/1³/₄ pints/4 cups lemonade or cream soda

1 Strip the redcurrants from their stalks with a fork. Reserve 50g/2oz/¹/₂ cup. Hull the strawberries and reserve 200g/7oz/1³/₄ cups.

2 Push the remainder through a juicer with the redcurrants. Pour into a glass punch bowl or jug (pitcher) and stir in the liqueur. Chill until ready to serve.

3 Halve the reserved strawberries and add to the juice with the redcurrants, plenty of ice cubes and the mint or lemon balm. Top up with lemonade or cream soda, and serve.

Nutritional information per portion: Energy 125kcal/524kJ; Protein 1g; Carbohydrate 22.6g, of which sugars 22.6g; Fat 0.1g, of which saturates 0g; Cholesterol 0mg; Calcium 40mg; Fibre 2.1g; Sodium 18mg.

Cuba libra

Rum and coke takes on a much livelier, citrus flavour with this vibrant Caribbean cocktail. The wonderful flavour and aroma of freshly squeezed limes dominate this blend, and the dark rum really packs a punch when combined with the sweet, syrupy cola drink.

MAKES 8 GLASSES

9 limes
ice cubes
250ml/8fl oz/1 cup dark rum
800ml/1¹/₃ pints/3¹/₂ cups cola drink

1 Thinly slice one lime then, with a citrus juicer, squeeze the juice from the rest. Put plenty of ice cubes into a large glass jug (pitcher), tucking the lime slices around them.

2 Add the lime juice to the jug, then the rum and stir with a long-handled spoon. Top up with cola drink and serve in tall glasses with stirrers.

COOK'S TIP
If you run short of limes, add some freshly squeezed lemon juice instead.

Nutritional information per portion: Energy 110kcal/461kJ; Protein 0g; Carbohydrate 10.9g, of which sugars 10.9g; Fat 0g, of which saturates 0g; Cholesterol 0mg; Calcium 6mg; Fibre 0g; Sodium 5mg.

Peach bellini

Try to serve this classic, fabulous cocktail only when peaches are at their most delicious and best. Preserved stem ginger and peach juice ice cubes make an unusual twist, so allow plenty of time for them to freeze before serving.

MAKES 8–10 GLASSES

75g/3oz preserved stem ginger (about 5 pieces), sliced
6 large ripe peaches
150ml/¹/₄ pint/²/₃ cup peach brandy or regular brandy
1 bottle sparkling wine

1 Place one or two slices of ginger in all the sections of an ice-cube tray. Halve and stone (pit) the peaches, then push through a juicer. Make 200ml/7fl oz/scant 1 cup of the peach juice up to 300ml/¹/₂ pint/1¹/₄ cups with water. Pour into the ice-cube tray. Freeze.

2 When frozen solid, carefully remove the ice cubes from the tray and divide among eight to ten wine glasses. Stir the brandy into the remaining peach juice, mix well and pour over the ice cubes. Top up with the sparkling wine and serve immediately.

COOK'S TIP
When the ice cubes start to melt, you will get an extra hit of peach and ginger juice in your drink. Drink this cocktail slowly to allow all of the flavours to merge. Also, if using both brandy and sparkling wine is too strong for your taste, top up with sparkling mineral water instead of wine. Alternatively, you can omit the brandy.

Nutritional information per portion: Energy 109kcal/453kJ; Protein 0.8g; Carbohydrate 8.4g, of which sugars 8.4g; Fat 0.1g, of which saturates 0g; Cholesterol 0mg; Calcium 11mg; Fibre 0.9g; Sodium 4mg.

Tropical storm

Whisky and ginger make a popular flavour combination in party drinks and cocktails, either served neat or blended with other ingredients to dilute the intense flavour. This refreshing creation with mango and lime has, unsurprisingly, plenty of kick.

MAKES 8 TALL GLASSES

2 large ripe mangoes
2 papayas
2 limes
150ml/¹/₄ pint/²/₃ cup ginger wine
105ml/7 tbsp whisky or Drambuie
ice cubes
lime slices and mango and papaya wedges, to decorate
soda water (club soda)

1 Halve the mangoes either side of the flat stone (pit). Using a spoon, scoop out the flesh from the halves and cut from around the stone using a small, sharp knife. Chop roughly.

2 Halve the papaya and discard the pips (seeds). Remove the skin and roughly chop the flesh. Cut away the skins from the limes and halve.

3 Push the mangoes, papayas and limes through a juicer. Pour into a jug (pitcher), add the ginger wine and whisky or Drambuie and chill until ready to serve.

4 Place plenty of ice cubes and long wedges of mango and papaya and slices of lime into tall glasses. Pour over the juice until the glasses are two-thirds full. Top up with soda water and serve.

Nutritional information per portion: Energy 127kcal/533kJ; Protein 0.6g; Carbohydrate 18g, of which sugars 17.9g; Fat 0.2g, of which saturates 0g; Cholesterol 0mg; Calcium 23mg; Fibre 2.6g; Sodium 7mg.

Grand Marnier, papaya and passion fruit punch

The term "punch" comes from the Hindi word panch *(five), relating to the five ingredients traditionally contained in the drink – alcohol, lemon or lime, tea, sugar and water. The ingredients may have altered somewhat over the years but the best punches still combine a mixture of spirits, flavourings and an innocent top-up of fizz or juice.*

MAKES ABOUT 15 GLASSES

2 large papayas
4 passion fruit
300g/11oz lychees, peeled and pitted
**300ml/¹/₂ pint/1¹/₄ cups freshly
    squeezed orange juice**
**200ml/7fl oz/scant 1 cup Grand Marnier
    or other orange-flavoured liqueur**
8 whole star anise
2 small oranges
ice cubes
**1.5 litres/2¹/₂ pints/6¹/₄ cups soda water
    (club soda)**

1 Halve the papayas and discard the seeds. Halve the passion fruit and press the pulp through a strainer into a small punch bowl or a pretty serving bowl.

2 Push the papayas through a juicer, adding 100ml/7 tbsp water to help the pulp through. Juice the lychees. Add the juices to the bowl with the orange juice, liqueur and star anise. Thinly slice the oranges and add to the bowl. Chill for at least 1 hour or until ready to serve.

3 Add plenty of ice cubes to the bowl and top up with soda water. Ladle into punch cups or small glasses to serve.

Nutritional information per portion: Energy 68kcal/284kJ; Protein 0.5g; Carbohydrate 9.3g, of which sugars 9.3g; Fat 0.1g, of which saturates 0g; Cholesterol 0mg; Calcium 15mg; Fibre 1.3g; Sodium 5mg.

Cherry berry mull

Inspired by the traditional warm spices used to flavour mulled wine, this sweet and fruity punch makes a novel drink for barbecues and summer parties. Nothing brings out the irresistible flavours of soft summer fruits quite like juicing, and the orange liqueur and spices add both a wonderfully rounded taste and a feisty kick to the drink.

MAKES 8 SMALL GLASSES

2 cinnamon sticks, halved

15ml/1 tbsp whole cloves

15g/1/2oz/1 tbsp golden caster (superfine) sugar

300g/11oz/2³/4 cups strawberries

150g/5oz/scant 1 cup raspberries

200g/7oz/scant 1 cup pitted cherries, plus extra to decorate

150g/5oz/1¹/4 cups redcurrants, plus extra to decorate

60ml/4 tbsp Cointreau or other orange-flavoured liqueur

extra cinnamon sticks for stirrers

1 Put the cinnamon sticks in a small pan with the cloves, sugar and 150ml/ 1/4 pint/2/3 cup water. Heat gently until the sugar dissolves, then bring to the boil. Remove from heat and leave to cool.

2 Push the strawberries, raspberries, cherries and redcurrants alternately through a juicer and pour the juice into a large jug (pitcher).

3 Strain the cooled syrup through a sieve (strainer) into the fruit juice, then stir in the liqueur. Serve in small glasses, decorated with cherries and redcurrants, and serve with cinnamon stirrers, if you like.

Nutritional information per portion: Energy 60kcal/253kJ; Protein 0.9g; Carbohydrate 10.4g, of which sugars 10.4g; Fat 0.1g, of which saturates 0g; Cholesterol 0mg; Calcium 16mg; Fibre 1g; Sodium 4mg.

Apple-spiced beer

Lager takes on a whole new dimension in this fun and fruity cooler. Diluted with freshly squeezed apple juice and flavoured with ginger and star anise, it's a great drink for anyone who wants to pace themselves through a party. The spiced apple juice can be made several hours in advance and chilled in a serving jug, ready for topping up at the last minute.

MAKES 8–10 TALL GLASSES

8 eating apples
25g/1oz fresh root ginger
6 whole star anise
800ml/1¹/₃ pints/3¹/₂ cups lager
crushed ice

1 Quarter and core the apples and, using a small, sharp knife, cut the flesh into pieces small enough to fit through a juicer. Roughly chop the ginger. Push half the apples through the juicer, then juice the ginger and the remaining apples.

2 Put 105ml/7 tbsp of the juice in a small pan with the star anise and heat gently until almost boiling. Add to the remaining juice in a large jug (pitcher) and chill for at least 1 hour.

3 Add the lager to the juice and stir gently to help disperse the froth. Pour over crushed ice in tall glasses and serve immediately.

Nutritional information per portion: Energy 42kcal/179kJ; Protein 0.3g; Carbohydrate 5g, of which sugars 5g; Fat 0.1g, of which saturates 0g; Cholesterol 0mg; Calcium 8mg; Fibre 0g; Sodium 7mg.

Mulled plums in Marsala

You needn't confine mulled drinks to the festive season. This fruity version, distinctively spiced and laced with Marsala, is served chilled, so it is perfect for drinks parties at any time of the year. It is also a delicious and practical way of using an abundance of sweet, juicy plums.

MAKES 4 GLASSES

500g/1¼ lb ripe plums
15g/½ oz fresh root ginger, sliced
5ml/1 tsp whole cloves
25g/1oz/2 tbsp light muscovado
   (brown) sugar
200ml/7fl oz/scant 1 cup Marsala
ice cubes

1 Halve two of the plums and discard the stones (pits). Roughly chop the remainder. Put the ginger, cloves and sugar in a small pan with 300ml/½ pint/1¼ cups water. Heat gently until the sugar has dissolved, then bring to the boil and add the halved plums.

2 Reduce the heat and simmer gently for 2–3 minutes until the plums have softened but still retain their shape. Using a slotted spoon, lift out the plums and leave them and the syrup to cool.

3 Push the remaining plums through a juicer. Strain the syrup and mix with the plum juice and Marsala. Put ice cubes and plum halves in four glasses and pour over the syrup. Serve with stirrers, if you like.

Nutritional information per portion: Energy 138kcal/583kJ; Protein 0.9g; Carbohydrate 21g, of which sugars 21g; Fat 0.1g, of which saturates 0g; Cholesterol 0mg; Calcium 23mg; Fibre 2g; Sodium 10mg.

Smoothies & juices basics

In this section you can learn about juicing and blending techniques and discover the best equipment to use for each drink. You'll also find out about the range of fruits and vegetables you can use, which ingredients work well together and how to get the most nutrients from your blend.

Getting equipped

For successful juicing and blending, you will need some basic equipment. The chances are that you will already have several items, such as a citrus press or a blender, but there are some more specialist items available that will make the job easier, quicker and much more fun.

Centrifugal juicers

Inexpensive yet perfectly adequate for most juices, centrifugal juicers have a collector for the fibre and pulp. Some also have an attachable jug (pitcher). These juicers grate very finely, spinning hard vegetables and fruit at great speed to separate the juice from the pulp. They are ideal for carrots, apples and leafy vegetables.

Masticating juicers

More high-tech and more expensive then centrifugal juicers, electric or manually operated masticating juicers finely chop the produce and force the pulp through a mesh to separate out the juice. They produce a greater volume of juice with more live enzymes. They can also be used to make nut butters, ice creams and healthy baby foods.

Food processors

These multi-functional machines comprise a main bowl and a variety of attachments, some of which you might have to buy separately. For making juices and blends, the most important attachments are: a strong blade, a centrifugal juicing attachment, a citrus attachment, whisking attachments and ice-crushing attachments.

Blenders

These feature a plastic or glass jug, with blades, placed on top of a motorized base. They work best with soft fruit, such as bananas, peaches and berries. Some can be used to crush ice, but check the instructions.

Citrus juicers

There are three main types of citrus press: electrically operated machines, which extract the juice into a container; manually operated hydraulic presses, which squeeze the juice into a container; and hand-operated squeezers, which collect the juice in the base and the pips in a ridge. They are perfect for all types of citrus fruit, though blenders, food processors or juicers retain the fibre and pulp of the fruit.

Electric wand

These handheld electric mixers are good for no-fuss blending. Some models come with a variety of attachments. You need to use an electric wand with a deep bowl, or a flask (which is sometimes supplied). If you are going to blend regularly, it is much more practical to buy a proper blender, although handheld wands can blend soft fruit and liquid, syrup or powdered ingredients well. Creamy whipped toppings can be made with the whisk attachment.

ABOVE: *Centrifugal (left) and masticating (right) juicers are quick and easy to use.*

RIGHT: *Citrus zesters and canelle knives are very useful items for preparing fruit.*

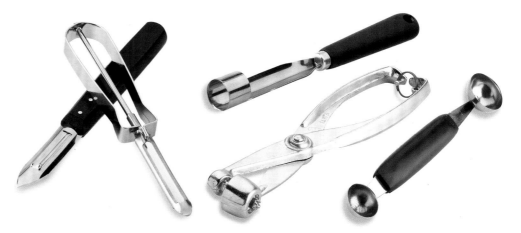

ABOVE: *There are many different types of vegetable peeler.*

ABOVE: *An apple corer, a cherry stoner and a melon baller.*

OTHER USEFUL EQUIPMENT

Chopping board

Plastic boards are easier to keep clean than wooden ones. Scrub with washing-up liquid and allow to air dry. Drying with a cloth often leads to recontamination. Always use one board for raw fruit, vegetables and bread, and another for meat.

Vegetable scrubbing brush

Use a firm brush to remove dirt from your vegetables.

Zester

A zester is extremely useful for grating rind and adding intense citrus flavour to juices and blends.

Canelle knife

This pares off the rind in ribbons or julienne strips. You can also buy combined zester/canelle knives.

Apple corer

These make quick work of coring apples or pears before blending. Place over the core at the stem end and push down firmly right through the fruit. Twist slightly and pull out the core and pips. There is no need to core apples or pears for juicing.

Sharp knife

A really sharp knife makes chopping easier and safer.

Plastic spatula

These are handy for scraping blends out of a blender or food processor, without scratching.

Cherry stoner

The easy way to pit cherries.

Melon baller

Use this small round scoop for neat balls of fruit.

Measuring jugs

A large jug, with measurements clearly marked, is a kitchen essential.

Sieve (strainer)

This can be useful when you want to strain juices to remove seeds and pips for fussy children, or if you just want a thinner juice.

Vegetable peeler

There are two main types of vegetable peeler: straight blade or swivel blade. Experiment to find the type you are most comfortable with, as it can make the job much easier.

Ice cream scoops

These are useful for scooping ice cream, frozen yogurt or sorbet into milkshakes or smoothies. Choose from half-moon-shaped stainless-steel scoops or spoon-shaped scoops with sleek steel or easy-grip plastic handles. Or you can try brightly coloured plastic scoops with quick-release levers.

Storage jug or vacuum flask

Choose a storage jug (pitcher) with a close-fitting lid or place clear film (plastic wrap) over the opening before securing the lid. Covering the juice or blend securely limits its exposure to oxygen and prevents it from oxidizing. Even better, use a wide-necked vacuum flask.

Serving jugs and glasses

Buy different shapes and colours and have some fun with them, contrasting them with the colour of the smoothie or juice you are serving.

Juicing and blending techniques

Once you have purchased the necessary equipment for juicing or blending, you will want to get started as soon as possible. For maximum freshness and flavour, prepare the fruit and vegetables just before you are ready to juice them. There are slightly different requirements for preparing produce for each type of machine. Before use, always read and follow the equipment manufacturer's instructions first.

Using centrifugal and masticating juicers

Although centrifugal and masticating juicers function in different ways, the preparation of fruits and vegetables, and the basic principles for using the machines, are much the same.

1 Always choose firm produce, not soft fruits, as soft fruits will not give successful results. For instance, firm, underripe pears work well, but soft, ripe pears are best prepared in a blender or food processor.

2 Prepare the produce. Most fruit and vegetables do not need to be cored or peeled – although you might prefer to core fruit – as peel, pips (seeds) and core will simply be turned into pulp in the machine.

3 Scrub clean with a hard brush any produce you are not going to peel. Use a little bit of soap or washing-up liquid to dissolve any waxy residue. Rinse thoroughly.

4 To remove the large stones (pits) of fruit, cut round the middle of the fruit with a small, sharp knife, then twist to break into two halves. Carefully ease out the stone with the knife. Mangoes have a large, flat stone. Peel the fruit, then cut the flesh away from either side of the stone. Remove as much flesh as possible from the stone.

5 All leafy vegetables, such as cabbages and lettuces, can be put through a juicer. Include the outer leaves, as they are nutritionally superior, but they must be washed thoroughly first.

6 Citrus fruit can be put through a juicer. Remove all the peel, but there is no need to remove the pips or pith.

7 When pushing the produce through the feeder tube of the machine, it is very important that you use the plunger provided. Remember to position a jug (pitcher) or glass under the nozzle of the machine to catch the juice, otherwise it will spray all over the work surface.

8 Always take care to chop and slice ingredients into manageable quantities before feeding them through the machine. Cut pears and apples into quarters, for example, and alternate them, if possible, to ensure that the juices mix well. If you push too many pieces of fruit or vegetable through the machine in one go, or push through pieces that are too large, the machine will get clogged up.

9 Push through a hard ingredient, such as a carrot or parsnip, after softer ingredients, such as cabbage. This will keep the juice flowing freely and will prevent blockages and damage to the machine.

Using blenders and food processors

These machines are very similar, and fruit preparation is the same for each. The main difference is the point at which you add liquid. Blenders and food processors are best used for soft fruits. As with any piece of electrical equipment, before you start to use any blender or food processor, always read the manufacturer's instructions first and follow them carefully.

1 Fruits with inedible skins, such as bananas, mangoes and papayas, should be peeled.

2 Fruits with edible skins, such as peaches or plums, do not need to be peeled but should be washed thoroughly. If you prefer a juice with a finer, smoother texture, peel the fruits before blending.

3 Fruits with large stones (pits), cores or pips (seeds), such as mangoes, plums, cherries and apples, should be stoned (pitted), cored or seeded.

4 Fruits with tiny seeds, such as raspberries, strawberries or kiwis, can be used whole, when the seeds add texture and a pretty speckled effect. However, if you prefer a smooth drink, the pulp can be pushed through a fine sieve (strainer), using a plastic spatula, to remove the seeds.

5 With berries and currants, remove the stalks and leaves and wash the fruit thoroughly. To detach, or string, redcurrants, blackcurrants or white-currants from their stalks, hold the bunch firmly at the top, then slowly draw the tines of a fork through the fruit so that the currants fall away.

6 To blend fruit in a food processor, place it in the bowl of the machine and process to a thick pulp. Add any liquid or creamy ingredient, such as water, fruit juice, milk or yogurt, and process again.

7 To blend fruit in a blender, it is important to add the liquid ingredients and the soft fruit at the same time, then process altogether, otherwise the blades will not be able to blend the fruits effectively.

8 If using a handheld electric wand, remember that this piece of equipment is not as powerful as other juicers or blenders. So use only very soft fruits, such as bananas, peaches and berries, as it cannot cope with anything firmer. It's also advisable that you only use it in shorter bursts.

Citrus juicers

1 First, cut the citrus fruit in half on a chopping board or plate using a small, sharp knife.

2 To use a traditional handheld juicer, press the cut half over the cone of the juicer and, using an even pressure all round, twist the fruit to squeeze out as much juice as possible. The rim of the squeezer will catch any pips (seeds) but you may need a bowl to catch the juice.

3 To use a juicer with a citrus attachment (which often come with blenders and juicers) or an electrically operated citrus juicer, firmly press the halved fruit over the spinning cone of the juicer. The motor will turn the cone under the fruit, and this will extract more juice than you would normally get with a handheld juicer.

4 To use a manual hydraulic press, place a container under the juice nozzle to collect the juice (unless one is supplied as part of the juicer) and place the halved citrus fruit in the press. Pull the lever forwards to apply pressure and squeeze out the juice.

5 To use a centrifugal or masticating juicer, remove the citrus peel with a sharp knife (don't worry about removing the pips or the pith). Cut the fruit into similar-sized chunks, then press through the juicer funnel.

Cleaning juicers, blenders and food processors

Possibly, the only dreary thing about making delicious juices and blends is that the equipment needs to be cleaned soon afterwards. However, there are some simple, no-fuss ways of making this chore much easier.

Cleaning a juicer, blender or food processor thoroughly is important to avoid unwanted and unhealthy bacteria. The best time is straight after you have made the juice or smoothie and poured it out. If you clean the parts immediately (or put them in to soak), the pulp and residue should rinse off easily.

1 Fill a sink with cold water and take the equipment apart, following the manufacturer's instructions.

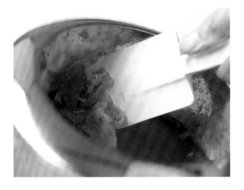

2 Using a plastic spatula or spoon, scoop off any large pieces of residue and discard it. Better still, if you have a compost heap in the garden, add the fruit or vegetable residue to it.

3 Plunge the non-electrical, removable machine parts of the juicer, blender or food processor into the sink full of cold water and leave

them to soak until you are ready to clean them – this will probably be after you've sat back and enjoyed your freshly made juice or blend. Soaking the machine parts will help to loosen any remaining fruit and vegetable pulp and will make cleaning them much easier.

4 After soaking, either handwash the non-electrical, removable machine parts or put them into a dishwasher on a normal setting.

5 Scrub any attachments that you have used with a firm brush to loosen any residue that remains. Take care when handling grating attachments as they are extremely sharp.

6 The removable components of your juicer, blender or food processor may occasionally get stained, especially if you regularly make juices with vibrantly coloured ingredients such as blackberries or beetroot. Soak these stained components every now and then in plenty of cold water with a little bleach added. Rinse the parts thoroughly afterwards, then leave until completely dry before putting the machine back together.

Troubleshooting

If you experience any problems using your juicer, or if the resulting drink is not quite what you imagined, the following may help.

The machine gets clogged up Push a hard fruit or vegetable, such as carrot or apple, through the machine to keep the juice flowing.

The taste of one ingredient is overwhelming the juice Increase the quantity of another ingredient. Use a base juice to dilute the flavours or add a splash of lemon or lime juice to help rescue the juice.

The blend is too thin Add an ingredient to thicken the drink, such as yogurt, cream, banana or avocado.

The blend is too thick Thin it using water or the juice of a watery fruit. For a pure taste, use fruit juice to dilute a fruit purée made in a blender.

The blend is too pulpy Strain through a sieve (strainer), pressing down with the back of a spoon.

The ingredients get stuck to the side of the bowl Scrape down the mixture with a plastic spatula to mix all ingredients thoroughly.

Citrus fruit

To juice citrus fruits, you will need a citrus juicer. The juice can then be added to other blends. Or, you can push the peeled fruit through a juicer to benefit from the fibre and pith. All citrus fruits are rich in vitamin C.

Preparing and juicing

To juice citrus fruits, you will need a citrus juicer (handheld, electric or hydraulic), a chopping board, a sharp knife, a scrubbing brush (for the rind) and a grater.

Juicing The simplest way to juice citrus fruits is to cut them in half and squeeze out the juice using a handheld juicer or a reamer. A hydraulic citrus press or citrus attachment on a citrus juicer will produce more juice. You can also use a food processor or blender.

Grating rind To use rind in a juice, choose a non-waxed organic fruit to avoid chemical residue or scrub the skin with a firm brush and a little soap, then rinse. Grate on the fine mesh of a grater or use a zester.

ORANGES

Choose eating oranges for juicing; Seville (Temple) oranges are too bitter. Blood oranges are sweeter than regular oranges and produce a lovely ruby-red juice. Orange juice goes well with most juices, particularly carrot, and is a good base for smoothies.

GRAPEFRUITS

Grapefruits range from bitter/sour to sour/sweet, and add a mildly sour note to sweeter juices, such as mango. Pink grapefruits are sweeter than yellow grapefruits.

LEMONS AND LIMES

These have a sour/bitter taste, so use only in small quantities. They are good with tomato juice, made into lemonade or limeade, or in a hot toddy.

MANDARINS, TANGERINES, SATSUMAS, CLEMENTINES AND TANGELOS

These mild, aromatic, sweet fruits make good base juices and combine well with tropical fruit.

BELOW: *Vibrant pink grapefruits are sweeter than yellow ones.*

LEFT: *Blends can be livened up with a fresh squeeze of lime juice.*

OTHER CITRUS FRUITS

Kumquats are fairly bitter, so juice with intensely sweet ingredients, such as apricots.

Mineola is wonderfully sweet, and so is perfect for juicing.

Pomelos are a good addition to mixed drinks that need sharpening.

Ugli fruit This fruit is delicious, mild, acid-sweet and juicy.

ABOVE: *A handheld juicer is the easiest way to squeeze the juice out of citrus fruits.*

ABOVE: *The zest of lemons works well with almost any ingredients.*

LEFT: *Buy oranges in bulk as they make a useful base juice.*

Exotic and other fruits

Most exotic fruits are now available all year round. These fruits are mainly blended because, apart from melons and pineapples, they will not go through a juicer very well.

Preparing and juicing

You will need a blender or food processor, a juicer (centrifugal or masticating), a chopping board, a sharp knife and a spoon (for scooping the flesh and seeds out of melons, kiwi fruit, papaya and guava).

Break peeled bananas into chunks for blending. With pineapples, use a large knife to slice off the base and the top. Cut into thick slices, then remove the skin. Put the flesh in a blender or food processor, or through a juicer. Peel lychees by hand; the skin is slightly stiff and cracks easily. Ease the fruit out and remove the stone. Put the flesh in a blender or food processor.

RIGHT: *Galia melon is delicious combined with either fruit or vegetables.*

ABOVE: *Pineapples can be mixed with most fruits.*

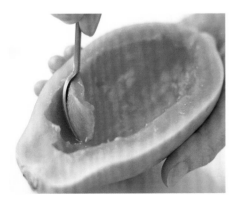

ABOVE: *Use a spoon to scoop out the flesh and seeds of papaya and guava.*

LEFT: *Ripe mangoes have extremely soft, sweet, juicy flesh.*

BANANAS

These make an excellent base for smoothies and combine well with many fruits, although not with vegetables. They are also a great, non-dairy way to thicken a blend.

PINEAPPLES

Once harvested, pineapples do not ripen further, so buy ripe fruit that is slightly soft to the touch and has a good colour with no green patches. The leaves should be crisp and green, with no sign of yellowing. Pineapple combines extremely well with most fruits and also with vegetable juices.

KIWI FRUIT

Tasting sweet, zesty and aromatic when ripe, kiwi fruit make a good base juice and combine well with other green fruits.

MANGOES, PAPAYAS AND GUAVAS

These aromatic, delicious and luxurious fruits combine well with banana and orange juice, apples or carrot to make tasty smoothies.

LYCHEES

Subtle, aromatic and sweet, lychees should be combined with equally delicately flavoured fruits. Use in smoothies with melons, bananas, apples or strawberries.

MELONS

The sweet, refreshing base juice of melon combines well with other fruits, such as tart apples or pears, or with bitter vegetables such as cabbage.

GRAPES

Though fairly watery, grapes work well with fruits that produce thicker juice, such as mangoes, papayas, peaches or plums. They work well with most fruit and vegetable juices.

Orchard and stone fruit

All of these fruits are rich in vitamins and minerals, with apricots being particularly high in betacarotene – a natural source of vitamin A.

Preparing and juicing

You will need a juicer for hard fruits, such as apples and pears, or a blender or food processor for softer fruits, such as peaches or plums. You will also need a chopping board, a sharp knife and a cherry stoner.

To use a blender Place the fruit in the goblet and add water, juice, milk or milk substitute. Cover and select the appropriate speed. To thicken, add banana, yogurt or cream.

To use a food processor Place the prepared fruit in the bowl, cover and select the appropriate speed. You can dilute the resulting pulp with water, apple or orange juice, milk or a milk substitute. If your food processor can crush ice, add some cubes at the end for a lovely fruit "slush" drink.

ABOVE: *Cherries are most easily pitted with a cherry pitter.*

APPLES

For juicing, choose eating apples, not cooking or crab apples. Apples are available all year round, making them ideal as a base juice. Apple juice oxidizes quickly to a brown colour but a little lemon juice will slow down this process.

While it may seem that choosing sweet apples is best, sharper-tasting eating varieties are often better because juicing concentrates the sweetness. They also balance out sweeter ingredients – for instance, sharp green apples work well to counterbalance the flavour of intensely sweet watermelon.

PEARS

These fruits have an aromatic scent and delicate flavour, which comes out particularly well when they are juiced. To fully enjoy their subtle flavour it

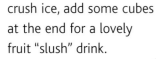

LEFT: *Aromatic pears make a subtle and refreshing juice.*

RIGHT: *Apricots make a deliciously thick and nutritious blend, perfect for a healthy breakfast juice.*

is best not to mix them with other very strong tasting juices, although they can be used to tone down the sometimes overwhelming flavours of cabbage and celery, for example.

APRICOTS

Ideally, choose tree-ripened fruit as the betacarotene levels increase by 200 per cent in the final ripening period. Blended apricots produce a thick, rich pulp that is best when diluted with juices such as cucumber, apple or carrot, or even sparkling mineral water. Add plain yogurt for a delicious smoothie. Dried apricots can be prepared in a blender with water.

CHERRIES

Choose ripe, sweet cherries for juicing as they do not ripen further after picking. They should be plump and firm, but not hard. Cherries lend a rich, aromatic flavour to juices and smoothies. Preparing them can be extremely time-consuming, and it helps if you have a cherry stoner to pit them. They are best used in small quantities with other blends and they turn juices and drinks a vibrant pinky-red colour. Cherry juice combines well with most other fruits and vegetables.

BELOW: *Juice from plums can be slightly sour if the fruit is underripe.*

ABOVE: *Nectarines do not need to be peeled before blending, but the large stone (pit) must be removed.*

ABOVE: *If you find fresh quinces, prepare and juice them as you would apples, then combine with very sweet fruit juices such as mango or peach.*

PEACHES AND NECTARINES

These fruits produce similar thick, sweet juices, though peach juice is slightly sweeter.

Peaches have a fuzzy skin, which you may prefer to peel off before juicing, but this is not necessary. With both fruits, you will get more juice using a blender or food processor rather than a juicer, and retain more of the fibre. If apricots are not in season, use peaches or nectarines.

PLUMS, GREENGAGES, DAMSONS AND PRUNES

Plums and greengages have a sweet, refreshing taste, although some varieties, especially when unripe, can be a little bit tart. Greengages are incredibly sweet and perfect for juicing, while damsons are fairly sour with a strong flavour, so are generally cooked with sugar before using. Prunes are dried plums and are intensely sweet – they can be blended with water to make a thick sweet juice, and they combine well with most citrus fruits.

Plums are best used with other, less sweet fruits or with more liquid ingredients, such as slightly sour apple juice. If a little underripe, plums will work well with bananas, mangoes or even orange juice.

QUINCES

Apple- or pear-like in shape, depending on the variety, and with a pale golden colour, quinces have a delightful scented taste when cooked. Eaten raw, they can be very astringent.

Quinces are hard when grown in cooler climates but ripen to a softer texture when grown in warm climates. For juicing purposes, quinces should be prepared like apples and juiced in the same way. They perfectly complement sweet peach or apricot juice.

Dried fruit

These are widely available and include raisins, sultanas (golden raisins) and currants, apricots, prunes, figs, mangoes, papaya, banana, apple rings and dates. Dried fruits do not juice well because they are dehydrated; however, they can be rehydrated by soaking in hot water, tea (Earl Grey is delicious), warmed wine or fortified wine. Adding cinnamon or another spice, such as cloves, complements their flavour. Dried fruits provide more concentrated sources of nutrients – including iron, magnesium and antioxidants – than their fresh equivalents. They are very sweet, so a little goes a long way in juices and blended drinks.

ABOVE: *Semi-dried apricots do not need soaking before use.*

Berries and currants

Ideal for smoothies and shakes. Raspberries and blackcurrants contain as much vitamin C as citrus fruits, while dark red berries also contain powerful antioxidants.

Preparing and juicing

You will need a blender or a food processor, a chopping board and a small, sharp knife.

Soft fruits Rinse, then discard any overripe or mouldy fruit. Remove stems and leaves, and the calyx from strawberries, though there is no need to hull them when making juices.

To use a blender Place the prepared soft fruits in the flask, add water, fruit juice, milk or milk substitute, cover and select the right speed. Add banana, other soft fruits, yogurt or cream to thicken.

To use a food processor Place the prepared fruit in the bowl, cover and process. To thin, add mineral water, orange juice, milk or a milk substitute.

ABOVE: *A small, sharp knife is essential for preparing soft fruits.*

STRAWBERRIES, RASPBERRIES, BLACKBERRIES AND MULBERRIES

Strawberries are at their best and sweetest when perfectly ripe. Wild strawberries are much smaller than cultivated strawberries and they are also expensive. Buy brightly coloured, plump berries and do not wash them until you are ready to use them.

Tarter than strawberries, raspberries are delicate, so handle with care, rinsing lightly, if necessary.

Try a classic strawberry milkshake or a raspberry and peach smoothie to sample these fruits at their best.

Blackberries usually arrive just as autumn is approaching. They grow wild in the countryside in abundance, but you can also find cultured blackberries in large supermarkets. Fully ripe, they are sweet and juicy.

Mulberries look a bit like blackberries in size and shape but they are less widely available. When ripe, they are sweet and slightly sour, and less aromatic than other berries.

When in season, if reasonably priced, use these fruits as a base juice. At other times, when the fruit is more expensive, just add a few berries to

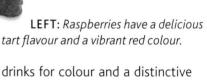

ABOVE: *Hunt for wild blackberry bushes, then pick your own.*

LEFT: *Raspberries have a delicious tart flavour and a vibrant red colour.*

drinks for colour and a distinctive taste. They blend well with bananas, orange juice, apples, melons, peaches and most other delicately flavoured fruits. Blackberries go particularly well with apples.

BLUEBERRIES

When ripe, blueberries (bilberries) are very sweet, but rather tart when underripe. Generally, they have a short summer season, except in warmer countries. Buy plenty and freeze them in small bags.

They are a delicious addition to most fruit blends, or you can just add sparkling mineral water to a thick blueberry purée.

BELOW: *Blueberries are a very potent antioxidant. They are good for boosting the immune system and play an important part in maintaining good eye health.*

BLACKCURRANTS, REDCURRANTS AND WHITECURRANTS

The general flavour of blackcurrants is sour-sweet, depending on their ripeness. They are best sweetened, although not if you are mixing a small amount of blackcurrant juice with a sweeter fruit juice. They make ideal mixers but are not good juiced on their own. Blackcurrants are more often made into cordials than into juices, and you could add some cordial to a juice made of other fruits.

Redcurrants and whitecurrants are less abundant than blackcurrants and difficult to find. They are good mixed with less expensive blackcurrants in juices and smoothies.

BELOW: *Whitecurrants are sweeter than other currants and less tart.*

BELOW: *Mix redcurrants with sweeter ingredients for a delicious blend.*

ABOVE: *Freeze gooseberries to use all year round.*

CRANBERRIES

These lovely winter berries are generally not available fresh at other times of the year. Buy when available and freeze. They are fairly sour and need sweetening. They work well with oranges, apples, pears or carrot (ratio: a quarter cranberry juice to three-quarters of the sweeter ingredient).

ELDERBERRIES

Not generally available in the shops, elderberries must be gathered wild. The elder tree grows widely and is found in many urban gardens, often disregarded as a weed. The berry is too tiny and sour for juicing, but makes an excellent sweet syrup when boiled with sugar and water. In spring and early summer, the flowers can be used to make a delicious cordial.

GOOSEBERRIES

These berries have a short summer season but can be frozen on baking sheets. They are rarely used for juicing because they can be extremely sour. However, you can add just a few to a juice to benefit from their immune-supporting effects.

Summer smoothies

When there is a glut of surplus berries but you don't want to freeze them, try making some of these classic berry smoothies.

- Raspberry and orange – this smoothie has a delicious tart flavour and is perfect for breakfast.
- Cranberry and pear – sweet and juicy pear contrasts with the slightly dry flavour of cranberries.
- Summer fruits – simply redcurrants, raspberries, strawberries and blackberries.
- Redcurrant and cranberry – a tart and refreshing smoothie, perfect on a summer's day.
- Raspberry and apple – kids will love this combination with plenty of crushed ice.
- Blueberry and orange – this smoothie will take on a vibrant bluish-purple colour.
- Blackberry and cinnamon – a warm, spicy blend guaranteed to impress your guests.

BELOW: *Tart blackcurrants contain more vitamin C than almost any other fruit, but they are best used in small quantities.*

Root and tuber vegetables

Though essentially autumn and winter vegetables, nutritious root and tuber vegetables are generally available all year round.

Preparing and juicing

To juice root and tuber vegetables, use an electric juicer, a scrubbing brush or a vegetable peeler, a chopping board and a sharp knife.
Peeling Many vegetables have nutrients just under the skin, so scrub rather than peel, unless really necessary, depending on skin thickness. Peel old carrots but not new ones or beetroot, celeriac, parsnips, radishes, swedes (rutabaga), turnips, sweet potatoes or yams. You can include potato skin, but cut away any peel or flesh that is sprouting or green as it can be toxic.
Juicing The foam at the top of vegetable juices can taste a bit earthy, but you should drink it for maximum benefit. If you don't like the taste, spoon it off, but do not strain the juice.

ABOVE: *Carrots make a sweet juice that works well as a base when combined with juice from other fruits or vegetables.*

CARROTS

These are the only root vegetables suitable for making a base juice. When juiced, carrots are very sweet and the fresh juice has a much better flavour than commercial carrot juice. Because they yield a lot of mild-tasting juice, carrots provide the basis for many combinations. They work very well with both vegetables and fruit.

BEETROOT

A rich ruby-red colour is imparted to drinks by the inclusion of beetroot (beet). Always used raw, they do not need to be peeled, just scrubbed. The juice is quite strong tasting, so use it sparingly: about one quarter beetroot juice to three-quarters other juice.

Beetroot greens enhance the nutritional value of the juice. However, they are fairly high in oxalic acid, which is poisonous if consumed in large quantities. Juiced beetroot and leaves work well in all vegetable combinations.

Beetroot is rich in betacarotene and other minerals, including iron and manganese. It is also traditionally used during convalescence.

BELOW: *Sweet, creamy parsnip juice should only be used in small amounts.*

ABOVE: *Root vegetables tend to produce a foam that settles at the top of juices.*

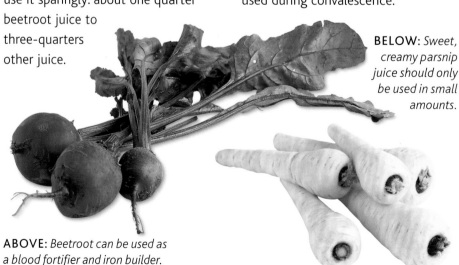

ABOVE: *Beetroot can be used as a blood fortifier and iron builder.*

PARSNIPS

This vegetable is high in sugar and so, like carrots, tastes fairly sweet. The juice is also quite creamy tasting. However, unlike carrot juice, parsnip juice should be added in smaller quantities – about one quarter parsnip to three-quarters other juice. It works best with other vegetable juices, especially slightly spicy, peppery ones.

RADISHES

These attractive vegetables come in a variety of shapes and sizes. They have a distinctive peppery taste, so use them in small quantities as a flavouring for other vegetable juices. They are ideal for bringing a bland juice to life.

SWEET POTATOES AND YAMS

Although these two vegetables look similar, they are not actually related and yams tend to be drier than sweet potatoes. There are many varieties of sweet potato, with flesh ranging from pale yellow to a vivid orange. Yam flesh varies from off-white, to yellow

ABOVE: *Yams have an alkalizing effect that helps overcome excess acidity.*

and pink, or even purple. Choose unblemished, smooth produce and store in a dark, cool, dry place.

CELERIAC, SWEDES AND TURNIPS

Celeriac has a mild celery taste; swede (rutabaga) is sweet and creamy but slightly earthy tasting; and turnips taste mild and peppery. Most of the nutrients in turnips are concentrated in the tops, so juice them along with the stems and leaves. All of these vegetables work best when added to other vegetable blends, for example in a

ABOVE: *Turnips are a good source of calcium and therefore a good nerve tonic.*

carrot-based juice with green leafy vegetables, but they do not combine particularly well with fruit.

POTATOES

Any type of potato can be used, but you must always use them raw in blended drinks. Potato has a slightly nutty flavour that is not unpleasant when mixed with other vegetable juices. It does, however, have good therapeutic effects, which makes it worth including. You only need a small quantity mixed with another juice, such as carrot, at a ratio of about one-eighth potato to seven-eighths other juice.

ABOVE: *The juice from potatoes is added to drinks for its therapeutic effect.*

ABOVE: *Peppery radishes should be juiced in small quantities only.*

Leafy and brassica vegetables

All dark-green leafy vegetables are good sources of magnesium and betacarotene, and many contain iron. They are also rich in compounds believed to have cancer-inhibiting properties.

Preparing and juicing

You will need a juicer (centrifugal or masticating), a chopping board and a sharp knife.

Loose, leafy vegetables Separate the leaves and wash thoroughly. Cut away discoloured leaves but keep the nutritious outer ones as well as lettuce cores and leaf stems.

Tightly packed leaves Wash vegetables such as chicory or Chinese leaves, then quarter or chop small enough to fit the neck of the machine. Cut broccoli and cauliflower into florets and wash thoroughly. The cores can also be juiced.

To extract the maximum juice Alternate putting leaves through the machine with hard vegetables or fruit.

ABOVE: *Separate loose, leafy vegetables and wash thoroughly.*

CABBAGES AND BRUSSELS SPROUTS

Dark-green cabbage is best for juicing as it is much more nutrient rich than white cabbage. When juiced, red cabbage will dominate your blend. Cabbage can lend a surprisingly light taste to juices but should not overwhelm the blend. About one-eighth to one-quarter cabbage is the right quantity in any juice. Brussels sprouts taste similar to cabbages when juiced, though slightly more nutty.

SPINACH

This has a mild, slightly peppery taste and lends a delightful green colour to

ABOVE: *Cabbage juice is a powerful gut and ulcer healer.*

juices. It is used in small quantities to add taste and nutrients to other sweeter bases, including milder fruits such as apples or pears.

ABOVE: *Known as a superfood, broccoli is packed with iron and vitamin C.*

RIGHT: *Brussels sprouts should be juiced in small quantities only as they have a strong, distinctive taste. Along with cabbages, they provide the richest vegetable sources of vitamin C.*

ABOVE: *Cauliflower, like broccoli, is a good source of vitamin K (see page 221).*

CAULIFLOWER AND BROCCOLI

These vegetables should have tightly packed, firm heads, with no sign of wilt or discoloration. They are both available in more exotic, expensive forms, such as purple sprouting broccoli and cauliflower hybrids, which can also be juiced. Broccoli

ABOVE: *Chinese cabbages make a change from the usual, while cavalo nero (black kale) is rich in magnesium, calcium and iron.*

tastes slightly bitter while cauliflower is creamy. Use in small quantities with milder flavours such as carrot or beetroot.

LETTUCE

There are many types of lettuce. The firm leaves juice better than the softer ones. Most varieties taste slightly bitter in juices, so use small quantities. Lettuce works well with vegetable or fruit blends.

KALE AND WATERCRESS

Both of these vegetables are strong tasting; kale is slightly bitter while watercress has a peppery flavour, so add only small amounts to juices. They are best used with other vegetable juices.

OTHER LEAFY VEGETABLES

There are many different types of leafy vegetables. Slightly bitter or peppery leaves include radicchio, rocket (arugula), Swiss chard, chicory (Belgian endive) and endive (US chicory). Use in small quantities, mixed with other vegetable juices. Sweeter-tasting leaves include Chinese leaves (Chinese cabbage) and pak choi (bok choy) – which combine well with vegetable and fruit juices.

WILD GREENS

When you are out and about, it is fairly easy to find dandelion, sorrel, nettles and, in some areas, watercress. Before gathering these plants, make sure you can identify them correctly and check that they have not been sprayed with weedkillers.

ABOVE: *All green-leafed vegetables are full of vital, health-giving minerals and nutrients. However, they are best mixed with other vegetables, as they are quite strong tasting on their own.*

Supertasters

It has been identified that at least one quarter of people are "supertasters" and have a very acute sense of taste, particularly for bitter and sour flavours. These people find that foods such as grapefruit, broccoli and Brussels sprouts are so bitter that they are unpleasant.

The result is that "supertasters" eat fewer vegetables to the point where it might impact on their health. Juicing is ideal for this group, as bitter tastes can be masked by sweeter and milder flavours from healthy sources.

Vegetable fruits

Some vegetables are actually the fruit of the plant. If allowed to ripen on the vine, they are all exceptionally nutritious.

Preparing and juicing

You will need a chopping board, a sharp knife, a spoon, a fork, a blender or food processor and a juicer.

Preparing avocados Avocado is ripe when the skin yields to pressure. Cut in half lengthways and ease the two halves apart. Scoop out the stone with a spoon, then the flesh, and place it in a blender or food processor with other ingredients.

Peppers Cut in half lengthways, then cut away the stem, pips and pith. Wash to remove any remaining pips, then push through a juicer.

Skinning tomatoes Place in a heatproof bowl and cover with boiling water for 2–3 minutes. Lift out, nick the skin with a knife and it peels back easily. Blend the tomatoes in a blender or food processor.

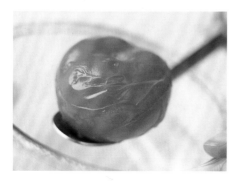

ABOVE: *Boiling water makes easy work of peeling tomatoes.*

AVOCADOS

When properly ripe, avocados are rich and slightly nutty tasting. They lend a creamy texture to juices and can be used to thicken a blend as an alternative to milk. They combine well with most vegetable juices – adding a little lemon juice will help cut through the richness and will slow down discoloration.

Avocados are an excellent source of oleic acid, which is good for the heart, and vitamin E, which is essential for healthy skin.

PEPPERS

Although they come in a variety of colours, (bell) peppers are all the same vegetable – green peppers are simply unripe red peppers. Peppers do not ripen much after picking, so they don't change colour or become sweeter. The taste of yellow, orange and red peppers is similarly sweet, while green ones have a slightly more bitter flavour.

Peppers can dominate a juice and so are best used in small

BELOW: *For the best flavour, store tomatoes at room temperature.*

BELOW: *Avocados contain plenty of vitamin E, making them good for the skin.*

quantities. They are ideal combined with tomato juice. Yellow, orange and red peppers also contain high levels of the antioxidant betacarotene.

TOMATOES

Mild-tasting tomatoes are sweet when ripe and acidic when unripe. Select vine-ripened tomatoes for the best flavour. Tomatoes mix well with most other vegetables and fruits. They are often used as a base juice as they are abundant and versatile.

Tomatoes are a rich source of lycopene, which has stronger antioxidant properties than betacarotene. They are also thought to have anti-cancer properties.

Squash vegetables

The high water content of these vegetables makes them ideal for juicing in a centrifugal or masticating juicer.

Preparing and juicing

You will need a juicer (either centrifugal or masticating), a clean chopping board and a sharp knife. **Preparing cucumbers and courgettes** Wash the skin, using a scrubbing brush if the vegetables are waxed. There is no need to peel or seed them, but do so if you prefer. Cut into large chunks and push through the juicer. You could also blend cucumbers in a blender or food processor as they contain so much water.

Juicing squashes Cut large squashes, such as butternut and pumpkin, in half and scoop out most of the pips, leaving some to go through the juicer, if you like. Slice away the peel, then cut the flesh into large chunks and push through the juicer.

ABOVE: *With large squashes, scoop out most of the pips before juicing.*

CUCUMBERS AND COURGETTES

When juiced, all cucumbers are mild and tasty, although small cucumbers have the best flavour. Ideal for using as a base juice, they mix well with both vegetables and fruit. Courgettes (zucchini) are similar to cucumbers when juiced, but not quite as sweet.

The nutrients of cucumbers and courgettes are mainly concentrated in the skin, which is why you should leave it on. These vegetables have a strong diuretic action, help to lower high blood pressure, support healthy hair and nail growth, and also help relieve the symptoms of rheumatism.

PUMPKIN AND BUTTERNUT SQUASH

Both of these squashes produce a juice with a surprisingly sweet and nutty taste, but it is not a juice that you would want to drink on its own. Mix one-quarter pumpkin or squash juice with three-quarters other vegetable juice, such as carrot or cucumber, along with something else to give it a bit of a zing – perhaps a bit of onion.

Include some of the pips in the juice as they are high in zinc and iron. These vegetables have a kidney-supporting and anti-water-retention action and are also powerhouses of carotenoid antioxidants.

ABOVE: *Courgette skin contains valuable nutrients, so don't peel before juicing.*

LEFT: *Pumpkins produce a sweet, nutty juice that is best mixed with other flavours for taste.*

Juicy soup

Raw vegetable juices can be used very successfully as soups. Either enjoy them cold in the summer, garnished with a dollop of cream or yogurt and chopped fresh herbs, or warm them through (but do not boil) in the winter months.

Gazpacho, which is made with raw tomatoes, cucumber and (bell) peppers, is the classic soup made in this way.

Pod, shoot and bulb vegetables

Because these vegetables are at the stage of growth before a fully fledged plant develops, they are highly nutritious and produce fairly strong-tasting juices.

Preparing and juicing

You will need a juicer, a chopping board and a sharp knife. Wash all vegetables thoroughly.
Preparing pods and bulbs French (green) beans, broad (fava) beans, runner beans and mangetout (snow peas) need only to be washed.

Pull off the outer leaves of bulbs, wash and cut into chunks, though not the outer leaves or skin from onions, spring onions, leeks, fennel or celery. Juicing shoots Cut the shoots from the roots of alfalfa and cress. Alternate shoot vegetables with hard vegetables, or else no juice will come out. Remove the woody stem of artichokes, cut the rest into chunks and push through the juicer.

ABOVE: *Peel the outer leaves and wash all vegetables thoroughly.*

BEANS AND MANGETOUT

Choose firm, crisp beans – choices include broad (fava), runner and French (green) beans. Avoid any that have been pre-trimmed or that are going soft. Buying local produce in season is the best option, because out of season beans are usually imported from countries where there might not be any regulations regarding chemical sprays. With the exception of mangetout (snow peas), which make a fairly mild and sweet juice, beans do not taste great when juiced – you will want to mix them with other vegetables.

FENNEL AND CELERY

These two bulb vegetables make very useful juices. Their tastes are fairly strong so they are best added to other juices, such as carrot, apple or pear, at a ratio of about one-fifth fennel or celery to four-fifths other

LEFT: *Fennel produces a strong aniseed juice that can be overpowering.*

ABOVE: *Leeks are a member of the onion family with similar healing properties.*

juice. Fennel tastes of aniseed, and juiced celery, when combined with other juices, does not taste as strong as the raw vegetable. Buy firm, pale green produce for the best flavours.

ONIONS AND LEEKS

All onions, including shallots, spring onions (scallions) and even red (Italian) onions, produce strong tasting juices. You only need to add a tiny quantity to a general vegetable juice. Leek juice is not as strong as onion juice but has a similar taste. One of the problems with onions, as with garlic, is that they can leave a residual taste on the mesh of the machine, meaning that extra cleaning is needed. Running half a lemon through the machine can help to mop up the scent.

ABOVE: *Mix asparagus juice with other vegetables for the best flavour.*

ASPARAGUS

A shoot vegetable, asparagus is available in the spring. It combines well with other vegetables but is not suitable to drink on its own.

The alkaloid asparagine, which is also found in potatoes and beetroot (beet), stimulates the kidneys but also turns urine a dark colour with a distinctive smell. This is not something to worry about, it is simply an indication of its diuretic effect.

BEANSPROUTS, CRESS AND ALFALFA

You can now buy beansprouts and cress in most large supermarkets, and alfalfa may be sourced in health food shops. Otherwise you can buy seeds and sprout them yourself (see below). They all give fairly strong tasting, peppery juices, so need to be mixed with other vegetable juices to tone down their flavour. They are probably easier to use in salads than in juices, but some people like to juice them for their distinctive taste.

GLOBE ARTICHOKE

The globe artichoke is actually a flower related to the thistle. The heart of the globe and the soft part of the petals attached to the middle are the parts normally eaten, but you can juice the whole vegetable, minus any woody parts.

ABOVE: *Beansprouts produce a distinctive, peppery juice.*

ABOVE: *The globe artichoke is often used to help with liver complaints.*

Sprout your own

Leguminous beans, pulses, lentils and peas are not suitable for juicing. However, they can be soaked and sprouted and then juiced.

1 Put one type of pulse in a large glass jar. Then pour in a generous amount of cold water and leave to soak for 24 hours. Discard the water, rinse the beans under cold running water and drain in a sieve (strainer).

2 Put the damp beans back in the jar. Cover with a square of cloth, securing with an elastic band.

3 Leave the beans in a dark, warm place and repeat the rinsing and draining twice a day for 3–4 days.

4 When the beans have sprouted, put them on a windowsill for 24 hours until the shoots turn green. They are now ready for juicing.

Natural flavourings and health supplements

Herbs and spices have been used for many years for flavouring food, and for their many health and healing purposes.

CULINARY HERBS

Most fresh herbs go well with vegetable juices. Put through a juicer with hard ingredients so that the machine does not become clogged up.

Basil

Pungent, aromatic basil is known as a soporific herb. Put it through a juicer

BELOW: *Basil can either be juiced or used as a tasty garnish.*

ABOVE: *If possible, pick fresh mint from your garden for the best flavour.*

or crush the leaves using a mortar and pestle. Or, make a tisane with hot water to add to juices or blends.

Mint

This prolific herb is a potent digestive aid. Flavours vary but all mints have a sweet aroma and cool aftertaste. Make a tisane and use to dilute juices.

Parsley

Of the two basic varieties of parsley – curly and flat leaf – the latter has the stronger flavour. Use sparingly. This herb is very rich in a number of nutrients, including calcium and betacarotene. Put through a juicer, followed by a hard vegetable, such as a carrot.

Chives

Members of the onion family, chives provide a mild onion flavour and have the same immune-supporting benefits as all types of leeks and onions.

Rosemary

This herb acts as a stimulant to the nervous and circulatory systems and is also thought to relieve indigestion. As an infusion, it is used to relieve colds and headaches.

Sage

This pungent herb effectively alleviates sweating as a side effect of menopausal hot flushes. Make a tisane with hot water and use to dilute juices. Do not use sage if breast-feeding as it can reduce milk flow.

BELOW: *Dill works well with carrot juice and aids digestion.*

Dill

With its distinctive yet mild caraway-like flavour, dill goes well with all green juices and carrot juice. It is also a soporofic and aids digestion.

ABOVE: *Rosemary aids indigestion and stimulates the nervous system.*

CULINARY SPICES

Culinary spices add great flavour to many juices and blends and have therapeutic benefits too.

Juniper berries

These berries' antiseptic properties can be used to treat urinary tract infections such as cystitis. Don't use if you are pregnant or have a kidney infection.

Horseradish

This pungent root is a potent sinus clearer. Grate a little for juices but do not put through a juicer.

Chilli

Whether mild or fiery hot, chilli spices reputedly support the immune system and see off colds and fevers. Use a tiny amount in vegetable juices but do not put through a juicer. Grind with a mortar and pestle. Avoid the seeds.

BELOW: *Root ginger is hot and spicy, so use it in small quantities.*

LEFT: *Grate a little horseradish into a juice to add extra spice.*

ABOVE: *Remove the seeds from chillies before juicing, unless you are a real fan of hot and spicy blends.*

Cumin

With the active compound curcumin, strong, nutty, yet slightly bitter cumin is an antioxidant-rich "super-spice". Dry-roast the seeds, then grind with a mortar and pestle to add to drinks.

Ginger

Fresh or ground ginger is pungent and quite hot. It lends itself to fruit and vegetable juices, particularly citrus fruits. The fresh root is best; otherwise add ground ginger or a supplement.

Nutmeg

Do not use too much of this sweet, aromatic, warming spice as it can have hallucinogenic effects.

Cardamom

These pods can help relieve vomiting and indigestion, sweeten the breath when chewed and treat colds.

Star anise

Use star anise, with its distinct aniseed flavour, to treat cramps and inflammation of the respiratory tract, loosen phlegm and calm peptic ulcers. Grind the seed and add to juices.

Cloves

The potent oil from cloves is often used to numb the gums during dental treatment or to relieve the pain for teething children. You can harness its strong antibacterial properties by making a tisane to add to drinks. Beware though – the flavour of cloves dominates other ingredients.

Cinnamon

A tree bark, cinnamon helps to soothe unsettled stomachs, can be used to revive the appetite, eases digestive tract spasms and alleviates flatulence. Grind the fresh spice and add half a teaspoon to juices or smoothies. The flavour complements banana, pear and carrot.

Garlic

This pungent bulb is regarded as a "super-herb" by juicing fans.

It is a potent blood thinner and immune-system supporter. It is best not to put it through the juicer as you will never get rid of the taste. Instead, pulverize it using a mortar and pestle and add just a tiny bit directly to the juice.

OTHER USEFUL HERBS, SPICES AND SUPPLEMENTS

It is easy to add medicinal herbs to blends and juices. Before you do so, however, make sure there are no contra-indications or interactions with any medications you are currently taking – check with your medical practitioner.

Chamomile

With its apple-like scent, yet pungent, bitter flavour, this calming herb is very safe, even for children. Use a chamomile teabag, available from larger supermarkets and health food shops, or simply infuse 4–5 fresh flower-heads and add the infusion to juice. Do not use if allergic to ragwort.

Ginkgo

Excellent for the circulation, ginkgo is also thought to be good for boosting memory. Empty a capsule into your blend and mix thoroughly.

Rosehip

The reddish-orange fruit of the rose contains high levels of vitamin C. Rosehips are usually sold as powder or tablets. Add a small amount of powder to

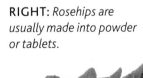

RIGHT: *Rosehips are usually made into powder or tablets.*

your blend (check the packet for quantities), crumble in a tablet or make a tisane to add to juices.

Ginseng

This sweet, liquorice-flavoured root is an energy booster and, some people believe, a libido enhancer. It is also reputed to relieve high blood pressure. It is available in health food shops. Simply empty a capsule or sprinkle some powder (according to instructions) into your blend.

Milk thistle

This important liver-supporting herb marries well with globe artichoke. It can help prevent alcohol-induced liver damage. Empty one or two capsules into your blend.

Liquorice

This root has a mild steroid effect and can help relieve the symptoms of most allergies. However, do not use alongside steroid medication or if you have high blood pressure as it can cause the retention of sodium and the depletion of potassium. It is available as a root from most health food shops. Grind the root with a mortar and pestle and sprinkle a little into your blend.

Echinacea

This is a classic immune-boosting herb often found as a supplement in fruit or herbal teas. It is usually taken in the winter to stave off cold and

LEFT: *Liquorice can help to relieve allergies.*

flu symptoms. Echinacea is widely available in tincture form and it is easy to add a few drops to your blend according to instructions, or you could make a tisane with hot water and add this to your drink.

Wheatgrass: a natural healer

A rich source of vitamins A, B, C and E, as well as all the known minerals, wheatgrass is a powerful detoxifier and cleanser. Its vibrant green colour comes from chlorophyll ("nature's healer"), which works directly on the liver to eliminate harmful toxins. Once juiced, wheatgrass should be consumed within 15 minutes, preferably on an empty stomach. Wheatgrass juice can be powerful in its effect, and some people may feel dizzy or nauseous the first time they drink it. Sip small amounts until your body gets used to it.

Adding supplements to juices is easy and beats popping vitamin and supplement pills every day. Before you do, though, check for contraindications.

Brewer's yeast

Rich in B-vitamins, and minerals such as iron, zinc, magnesium and potassium, Brewer's yeast also supplies protein. Its strong taste becomes pleasantly nutty when blended with fruits or vegetables.

Bee pollen

This is a useful immune booster and can also help relieve the symptoms of hay fever.

Spirulina and wheatgrass

Both spirulina and wheatgrass are often used in supercharged, healthy juices. They are readily available in powdered form or you can grow your own.

Kelp

This form of seaweed is very rich in calcium, copper, iron, magnesium, potassium, zinc, B vitamins and betacarotene. It also contains high

RIGHT: *Kelp is a form of seaweed and is packed full of vitamins and minerals.*

levels of iodine, which is vital for the normal functioning of the thyroid gland, but do not take if you have an overactive thyroid. It is also used to treat common colds, constipation, arthritis and rheumatism.

Sambucol (elderberry extract)

During the winter when berries are not readily available, add a teaspoonful of sambucol to juices. This rich source of proanthocyanins will boost your immune system.

Aloe vera

Aloe vera provides two main products: aloe vera gel, which is used externally for soothing skin irritations and sunburn, and aloe vera juice, which can be added to your juices and blends. Aloe vera juice is reputed to help relieve the symptoms of arthritis, ME and eczema, and is also renowned for soothing and rebuilding the digestive tract. Choose a certified product with a guaranteed amount of active compounds and add a dose, according to the instructions on the packet, to your blend.

FATS AND OILS

Healthy fats are good sources of essential fatty acids, which can help to clear up a range of complaints including dry skin, listless hair and low energy levels.

Lecithin

Add 5–10ml/1–2 tsp of lecithin, an emulsifier derived from soya, to the ingredients in a blender before any fats. It helps fat digestion.

Evening primrose oil

This can be helpful in alleviating pre-menstrual problems and allergies. Pierce a capsule with a pin and squeeze into your juice or blend.

Walnut oil

Pleasant and light, walnut oil is a good source of both omega-3 and omega-6 fatty acids, which are useful for nervous and hormonal health. Add 5–10ml/1–2 tsp to a glass of juice. Store in the refrigerator.

Flax seed oil

A "super-oil", this has high levels of omega-3 fatty acids. Add 5–10ml/1–2 tsp to your juice. Store in the refrigerator.

RIGHT: *Walnut oil has a pleasant nutty flavour that works well in most juices because it does not overwhelm them.*

Nuts and seeds

*These powerhouses of
nutrition are excellent
sources of protein, fibre,
vitamin E, zinc, iron,
selenium, magnesium and
calcium. They also provide
essential fatty acids.*

NUTS

Choose whole unsalted nuts to make
blends and smoothies, and always
check the expiry date on the packet.
After opening a packet, store any left
over in a glass jar with a screwtop lid
in the refrigerator to keep them fresh.
Choose from walnuts, Brazil nuts,
pistachio nuts, pecan nuts, hazelnuts
or almonds to add flavour and crunch

ABOVE: *Walnuts are believed to help
prevent heart disease when eaten as a
regular part of your diet.*

to blended drinks. Peanuts are not
really nuts but legumes, a member
of the bean family, which is a part
of the reason why some people are
allergic to them.

You could use various smooth nut
butters, which are available from
supermarkets or health food shops,
to flavour drinks instead of whole
nuts. Add them directly to the blend
and mix thoroughly. Delicious nut and
seed milks, such as almond milk
(see right) are easy to make at
home and can be used to
give smoothies or milkshakes
an intense, nutty taste.

Nuts can have important
therapeutic benefits when used to
replace other fatty ingredients in the
diet. For instance, if you eat walnuts
regularly, this can help to reduce the
risk of heart disease.

ABOVE: *Pecan nuts combine particularly
well with banana, while pistachio nuts add
a delicate green colour to blends .*

MAKING ALMOND MILK

This method can be used for almost
any other nuts and seeds as well as
almonds.

1 In a heatproof bowl, cover
115g/4oz/1 cup whole almonds
with boiling water and leave to
stand for 5 minutes. Drain and
discard the water.

2 The skins will now be loose.
Squeeze the almonds gently out
of their skins.

3 Place the skinned almonds in a
blender with 250ml/8fl oz/1 cup
water and blend roughly.

4 Add another 250ml/8fl oz/1 cup
water and continue blending until
you achieve the consistency of
a thick paste.

5 Gradually add more water until
you achieve the consistency you
require – somewhere between
cream and milk.

6 Blend until there is no residue
remaining or strain the almond
milk to remove any residue.

SEEDS

Buy seeds ready hulled in small packets and keep them as you would nuts. Choose from pumpkin seeds, sunflower seeds, pine nuts, linseeds (flax seeds) and sesame seeds.

Coconut is not really a nut, but a huge seed. It is high in saturated fats so it is best to limit the amount of coconut flesh or milk you use. Linseeds (flax seeds) are particularly rich in an important member of the omega-3 family of fatty acids. The culinary oil derived from linseeds is called flax seed oil. Sesame seeds are made into a thick, rich-tasting purée called tahini, which can be added in small amounts to blended drinks. Dark tahini, which uses the whole seed including the husk, is about ten times richer in calcium than light tahini, and turns it into a calcium-match for milk.

ABOVE: *Coconut is delicious but very high in saturated fat.*

RIGHT: *Despite their name, pine nuts are actually a seed.*

GRAINS AND FIBRE

When making juices and blends it is easy to sneak in extra healthy ingredients. Grains are excellent sources of B-complex vitamins, vitamin E, calcium, magnesium, iron, zinc and essential fatty acids.

Wheatgerm This comes as a coarse powder and it is easy to add 5ml/1 tsp to a smoothie blend.

Oatmeal Choose fine-ground oatmeal and add 10–15ml/2–3 tsp to a blend, or to milk with some honey for a night-time drink. Oatmeal provides gentle soluble fibre, which is important for reducing cholesterol levels.

Rice You can use rice as a thickener for smoothies or shakes if you are allergic to wheat. Cooked pudding rice works well.

LEFT: *Wheatgerm is an excellent source of vitamin E. You can add wheatgerm powder to your blends in small quantities.*

RIGHT: *Pudding rice works well as a thickener for blended drinks.*

Bran and psyllium While psyllium can be bought only from health food shops bran is widely available. Oatbran contains soluble fibre, which can help to reduce cholesterol levels. People suffering from constipation are often tempted to try wheat bran, though some find it too abrasive. Instead, try adding 5–10ml/1–2 tsp of psyllium to a blend.

Dairy and dairy alternatives

Adding milk, yogurts, dairy or milk substitutes to blended drinks results in a more luxurious and creamy, though not necessarily more fattening, treat. Milk is calcium rich (even skimmed milk) and many milk alternatives are now enriched with calcium.

MILK

For a rich and creamy taste choose full cream (whole) milk. Most people, however, need to avoid too much saturated fat in their diet and would be better advised to use skimmed or semi-skimmed (low-fat) milk.

Milk is one of the richest sources of calcium available. Full cream milk is only usually advised for young children, who need the calories it provides to promote growth and bone health.

CREAM

For extra indulgence, use double (heavy) or single (light) cream, crème fraîche, mascarpone, smetana or, for a different taste, sour cream.

Cream is an excellent source of vitamin E, which helps to maintain healthy skin, but it is also very high in calories so it should only be used in moderation.

YOGURT

For making shakes or smoothies thicker, yogurts are an extremely useful ingredient. Greek (US strained plain) yogurt is much thicker than standard varieties but has almost as many calories as cream, so it should not be used on a regular basis. Low-fat yogurts, including low-fat Greek yogurt, are readily available instead, so you can still indulge yourself without feeling too guilty. Fruit yogurts can add interesting flavours to fruity blends.

Yogurt is rich in calcium and is often suitable even for people who have a milk intolerance. Choosing to eat live "bio" yogurt as a regular part of your diet can help improve digestive tract health by providing healthy bacteria. High-fibre yogurts that have cholesterol-lowering properties are also now widely available in shops and supermarkets.

Alternative milks

Often used by people who have a dairy allergy, alternative milks are a good low-calorie option. The fats in most nut milks, except for coconut, are healthy polyunsaturated fats.

Soya milk Choose the calcium-enriched variety of soya milk if you are using it instead of cow's milk on a regular basis.

Rice milk This has a thinner and lighter consistency than cow's milk, but a deliciously sweet flavour. Vanilla- and chocolate-flavoured rice milks are also available.

Oat milk This alternative to cow's milk is extremely rich and has a creamy, smooth taste.

Nut milks Coconut milk is delicious but, due to its rich flavour, it is best diluted or used in small amounts. You can now buy almond milk and other nut milks from most large supermarkets or health food shops.

BELOW: *Many low-fat alternative milks are now calcium-enriched.*

BELOW: *Natural yogurt is ideal, but try experimenting with low-fat varieties.*

FROZEN INGREDIENTS

Ice creams, sorbets (sherbets), frozen yogurts and soya ices can all be scooped straight from the freezer to make a delicious old-fashioned shake. Although a good source of calcium, dairy ice cream is high in calories. Non-dairy ice creams and sorbets do not have the benefit of calcium.

LOW-FAT CREAMY INGREDIENTS

Fromage frais (cream cheese) and plain cottage cheese can both be bought in low-fat versions and used as creamy thickeners, as can buttermilk, which tastes slightly sour. These are perfect for anybody on a calorie-controlled diet.

TOFU

Also known as soya bean curd and beancurd, tofu is available in firm, medium-firm and silken varieties.

ABOVE: *Tofu is rich in hormone-balancing phytoestrogens, which can help protect against some cancers.*

A fairly bland food with a slight nutty taste, it will affect the texture of drinks, but not the taste. Soft, silken tofu is best for blending and adds a creamy thickness to the blend.

Tofu is an all-round healthy food – high in protein, low in saturated fats and calories, easy to digest and cholesterol free. It has high levels of calcium and vitamin E, which helps to maintain healthy skin and protect against heart disease.

BELOW: *As an occasional treat, you can use real strawberry ice cream to make a traditional milkshake. Remember, though, that dairy ice cream is high in calories, so it's best not to overdo it if you're watching your weight.*

EGGS

Raw eggs contain high levels of vitamin B12, which is vital for the nervous system. Eggs are often used as the basis of protein shakes by sports enthusiasts or in hangover remedies to kick-start the system. Before using raw eggs in a blend, you should be aware of the following:

• Raw egg white binds with the B-vitamin biotin and, if overused, can lead to a deficiency of this nutrient.
• Pregnant women, children, the sick or elderly, or those with an impaired immune system should not eat raw eggs because of the risk of salmonella.
• Eggs have a high cholesterol content – in the yolk. People with high cholesterol may benefit from limiting their weekly intake of eggs to five. However, as most cholesterol is made in the body, and this is adversely affected by a high saturated fat intake, it is better to reduce saturated fats from butter, cheese and meat.
• Eggs containing high levels of omega-3 fatty acids are now widely available, and could help maintain a healthy heart.

BELOW: *Raw eggs can thicken blends nicely but it is not safe for everybody to eat them.*

Sweeteners and other flavourings

One big advantage of juices and smoothies is that it is occasionally possible to indulge a sweet tooth and still benefit from the healthy basic ingredients.

SWEETENERS

Many juices, whether made from fruit or vegetables, are naturally very sweet, so you may need to dilute them slightly. Try adding one-third to one-half water – either still or sparkling. You can also add a variety of milky ingredients. Adding water or milk will ensure that blood sugar levels rise more slowly. Children should always drink juices diluted to reduce the impact on their teeth.

If a juice, smoothie or milkshake is not sweet enough, simply add some sugar – white, brown or muscovado (molasses) – or flavoured syrups, such as vanilla, or fruit cordials. There are, however, many other sweeteners that you could use.

Honey

Different honeys have varying tastes, depending on the type of pollen gathered. Popular choices are lavender or apple blossom honey, which have a fragrant sweetness. Manuka honey is renowned for its health-promoting properties; it is anti-bacterial, making it ideal for sore throats. Honey should not be fed to children under the age of 12 months as it could cause botulism, a type of food poisoning that can be fatal.

Fructose

Instead of using table sugar (sucrose), you could use fructose (a natural fruit sugar). This has a lower Glycaemic Index (GI) score than sucrose so can be used in moderation by people with diabetes. (GI is a measure of how quickly a carbohydrate enters the blood stream as sugar. The higher the score, the less healthy the carbohydrate.)

Fructose is sweeter than table sugar so do not substitute directly in drinks.

Blackstrap molasses

During sugar refining, the juice squeezed from the cane or beet is boiled until syrupy and then the sugar crystals are extracted. There are three boilings, resulting in light molasses, then dark and finally blackstrap molasses, which is thick, dark and rather bitter. It is a rich source of calcium, iron and magnesium but only a little should be used.

FOS (Fructooligosaccharide)

A natural fibre found in bananas, Jerusalem artichokes, tomatoes, onions and other fruits and vegetables, FOS looks like sugar and is almost as sweet, but does not affect blood sugar levels. It is found in health food shops. A moderate amount promotes the growth of good bacteria, benefiting the digestive tract. Too much FOS can lead to bloating.

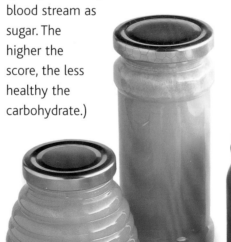

ABOVE: *Choose from many different flavours and types of honey.*

ABOVE: *Blackstrap molasses is intensely sweet and so only a tiny bit is needed.*

OTHER FLAVOURINGS

Many other ingredients and sweet additions can be included in smoothies. Health-promoting properties become less important here – everyone deserves to indulge themselves occasionally.

Coffee

Freshly ground or instant, coffee is just the thing if you need a wake-up call with your morning blend. Try adding it to creamy blends to make a coffee-flavoured smoothie or shake. Use decaffeinated coffee if you are caffeine sensitive and, if you are feeling particularly virtuous, try using dandelion coffee, which is reputed to have liver-cleansing properties.

Chocolate

This is an irresistible ingredient, whether melted, grated or in powder form. Dark (bittersweet) chocolate is the best for you as it is rich in iron and antioxidants, but for a milder flavour you should use milk chocolate. For a decadent finish, grate or shave chocolate on top of your smoothie – dark, plain (semisweet), milk or white, whichever you prefer.

Sweets (candies)

Try adding sweets to the side of the glass as a decoration that is guaranteed to impress at a kid's party, or add them to the blender and blend them into the drink. Turkish delight or nougat are good choices, or you could serve a smoothie with an edible swizzle stick in the shape of a chocolate wand.

ABOVE: *Create a traditional, decadent milkshake with rich, dark chocolate.*

BELOW: *Try crumbling brownies on top of your favourite chocolate milkshake.*

Cakes and cookies

Brownies or meringues can be crumbled on top of smoothies or added to the blend for texture, and any other cakes or cookies can be used instead if they complement the drink you are serving. Amaretti provide a lovely almond accent, for example, which would be delicious with strawberry, apricot or peach-based blends, or try crunchy coconut macaroons sprinkled on top of a tropical fruit blend.

ABOVE: *When added to your blends, meringues give an irresistible crunch.*

BELOW: *When adding alcohol to your punchbowl, you only need a small amount.*

Alcohol

Add a splash of alcohol to your favourite drinks when you want to relax with a smoothie at the end of the day, or give your party juices a boost. Choose different drinks for their flavours, such as coffee, mint, or orange liqueurs – or experiment with other more exotic liqueurs. If you want to give your blend a real kick, you could even try a shot of brandy or whisky.

Juicing for a healthy diet

Juicing as part of a healthy lifestyle, involving a balanced diet and regular exercise, can help to ensure optimal energy levels, a zest for life and, of course, general good health.

Therapeutic juicing

To get the therapeutic benefits from juices, you need to have them regularly, preferably daily. Drinking juices will also keep you rehydrated and help you get your recommended five portions of fruit and vegetables a day. Remember: therapeutic juicing works by supplementing – not replacing – a healthy, balanced diet.

Immune system health and allergies

Carrots, cantaloupe melons, cherries, blueberries, blackcurrants, kiwi fruit, grapes, watermelons and tomatoes all help support the immune system.

Broccoli, cabbage, Brussels sprouts and cauliflower are thought to be potent cancer fighters. Garlic, onions and leeks fight off colds, coughs and flu, and quince aids convalescence.

People with allergies benefit from their five a day; dark red and purple berries seem particularly effective.

Respiratory health

Apples, onions and dark red and purple berries strengthen the lungs.

Reduce catarrh by avoiding dairy products and using garlic. Turnips have expectorant properties, and radish and horseradish help to clear the sinuses. Nettles may alleviate hayfever symptoms.

Cleansing and urinary tract health

Apples, strawberries and grapes are good for general detoxing.

Globe artichoke, lemon, cranberry and fennel support the liver. Radish is good for the gall bladder.

ABOVE: *Quercitin, found in onions, is good for the lungs.*

Celery, cucumber, cranberry, dandelion, celeriac, fennel, strawberry, peach and watermelon have a diuretic action and stimulate the kidneys, as does asparagus, which helps to purify the blood.

Cranberry and blueberry juice and garlic are good for cystitis and other urinary infections.

Digestive health

For constipation and diarrhoea, add 5–10ml/1–2 tsp ground linseeds (flax seeds) or 5ml/1 tsp psyllium husks to a drink daily. Plums, prunes, peaches,

Healthy and balanced
For a healthy, balanced diet, follow these simple rules:

1 Eat at least five portions a day of fresh fruit and vegetables.

2 Eat a wide variety of fresh foods to make sure you get all the vitamins and minerals you need.

3 Base your diet on fruits, vegetables, grains, legumes, nuts, seeds and eggs. If you are a meat-eater, always select lean cuts and restrict your intake of red meats. Fresh, unprocessed fish is generally a healthier option.

4 Keep processed, salty, sugary or fatty foods to a minimum.

5 Drink sufficient water to stay hydrated: 1.5–2 litres/2½–4 pints/1½–2 quarts per day is the usual recommendation.

ABOVE: *Apples are useful for aiding digestion and cleansing the liver.*

nectarines, figs and pears are good laxatives. Ginger aids nausea and morning sickness.

Apples help to normalize digestive function and improve liver function. Fennel juice is excellent for most digestive conditions. Pineapples and papayas aid indigestion, impaired digestion and stomach ulcers, as do potato juice and cabbage, which also help to heal the gut wall.

Rich in fibre, all fruits and vegetables are good for bowel health. Smoothies rather than juices will increase your fibre intake.

Circulation and blood health

Dark-green leafy vegetables may help prevent osteoporosis. Citrus fruits support healthy blood vessels and prevent varicose veins.

Raw beetroot (beet), dandelion juices and dark-green leafy vegetables combat anaemia. Combine with citrus juice or tomato juice for improved iron absorption. The potassium in all

fruit and vegetables helps to lower blood pressure. Watermelon, cucumber, grapes and bananas are especially good sources.

Reproductive and sexual health

The zinc in nuts and seeds is essential for healthy sperm. For women, the folic acid in green leafy vegetables and citrus fruit is vital preconceptually and in the first trimester. Warm ginger and ginseng can revitalize the libido. Women with perimenopausal symptoms can try adding 50–90g/2–3$\frac{1}{2}$oz silken tofu or 300ml/$\frac{1}{2}$ pint/1$\frac{1}{4}$ cups soya milk to drinks on a daily basis for valuable phytoestrogens, which mimic the action of oestrogen.

Skeletal and muscular health

All types of magnesium-rich green leafy vegetables, nuts and seeds help calcium utilization in bones. They are also good for alleviating muscular cramps, including menstrual cramps.

Cucumber juice, cherry, grape, pineapple and dandelion help to

combat rheumatoid arthritis, while elderberry juice eases rheumatic pain.

Milk, yogurt or calcium-enriched alternative milks provide calcium; Vitamin D is made in the skin and is vital for calcium use by bones. The best source is half an hour of sunlight each day, spring and summer. If convalescing or susceptible to osteoporosis, add vitamin D supplement to a juice every day.

Mental and nervous health

Turnip, dandelion and beans are good nerve tonics, celery is restful, and lettuce and oatmeal promote sleep.

A lavender tisane soothes headaches, as does fennel (even migraines). Potato juice relieves nervous eczema. Vitamin B-rich wheatgerm, brewer's yeast, yogurt, vegetable extract, molasses, peanut butter, oranges and other citrus fruits, sweet potatoes and broccoli aid mood and memory.

Green leafy vegetables, nuts and seeds, blackcurrants, citrus fruit, strawberries, Brussels sprouts and peppers help to relieve stress.

ABOVE: *Seeds are rich in magnesium, which helps maintain healthy bones.*

Vitamins and minerals

Drinking fresh juices and blends made from fruits and vegetables is an excellent way to get your recommended daily allowances (RDAs) of vitamins and minerals.

VITAMINS

Vitamin A – retinol

Essential for: healthy eyes, skin and mucous membranes. Retinol is available only from animal sources, such as full cream, oily fish and liver, and large amounts can be toxic. Betacarotene converts to vitamin A

ABOVE: *Broccoli juice is packed with essential minerals and vitamins.*

only as it is needed, and is non-toxic.
Juicing it: orange-coloured fruit and vegetables; and dark-green, leafy vegetables.

Vitamin B1 – thiamine

Essential for: energy and to support the nervous system.
Juicing it: cauliflower, pineapple, orange, leek, brewer's yeast and peanuts.

Vitamin B2 – riboflavin

Essential for: energy production; healthy skin, hair and nails.
Juicing it: broccoli, apricots, spinach and watercress; brewer's yeast; milk, yogurt and cottage cheese.

Vitamin B3 – niacin

Essential for: energy production and feeling calm.
Juicing it: potatoes, beansprouts, strawberries, parsley, peppers, avocados, figs, dates and wheatgerm.

Vitamin B5 – pantothenic acid

Essential for: energy production and counteracting stress.
Juicing it: broccoli, berries, watermelon, celery, sweet potatoes, wheatgerm, brewer's yeast, vegetable extract, molasses and nuts.

Vitamin B6 – pyridoxine

Essential for: processing protein, healthy nervous and immune systems, and healthy skin.
Juicing it: oranges, brassicas, bananas, potatoes, yam, watermelon, pumpkin seeds and wheatgerm.

Vitamin B12 – cobalamine

Essential for: metabolizing iron and a healthy nervous system.
Juicing It: vegetable extract; milk, yogurt and cottage cheese.

Folic acid

Essential for: preconception and healthy early pregnancy; works best with B12 and B6.
Juicing it: citrus fruits, broccoli, Brussels sprouts, lettuce, potato, beetroot (beet), apricots, pumpkin, peanuts and almonds.

Vitamin C – ascorbic acid

Essential for: immunity, bone health, skin repair, aiding recovery, iron absorption, and protecting against heart disease and cancer.
Juicing it: raspberries, strawberries, blackcurrants, citrus fruits, papaya, kiwi fruit, beetroot (beet), tomatoes, peppers, cabbage, cauliflower, watercress and potatoes.

Vitamin D

Essential for: healthy bones and teeth, and protecting against breast and prostate cancer. It is mainly made by the skin when exposed to the sun. Half an hour per day on face, hands and arms is recommended. Dietary sources are oily fish, such as mackerel and salmon, and margarines.
Juicing it: there are no food sources of vitamin D to add to juices.

Vitamin E

Essential for: protecting against heart disease and ageing, and to thin the blood.

Juicing it: all nuts and seeds and their oils, dark-green leafy vegetables, cream and wheatgerm.

Vitamin K

Essential for: healthy blood clotting, wound repair and healthy bones.
Juicing it: leafy vegetables, especially cauliflower, and yogurt for healthy gut flora, which make vitamin K.

MINERALS
Calcium

Essential for: healthy bones, muscles, heart and blood clotting.
Juicing it: broccoli, cabbage and kale; milk and other dairy produce (not butter or cream); soya milk, rice milk and tofu.

Chromium

Essential for: regulating blood sugar levels.
Juicing it: carrots, cabbage, lettuce, oranges, apples, bananas and milk.

Iodine

Essential for: thyroid health, metabolism, energy and mental function.
Juicing it: vegetables grown in iodine-rich soil, kelp and milk.

Iron

Essential for: making blood and delivering oxygen to cells; energy and mental function.
Juicing it: dark-green leafy vegetables, dried fruits, nuts, seeds, molasses and dark chocolate; uptake of iron from plants is doubled when taken with juices rich in vitamin C.

Magnesium

Essential for: healthy bones; works in synergy with calcium.
Juicing it: green leafy vegetables, potatoes, citrus fruits, dried fruit, nuts and seeds.

Manganese

Essential for: metabolism of fats and carbohydrates.
Juicing it: green leafy vegetables, peas, beetroot (beet) and nuts – which you can add to blends and smoothies.

Phosphorus

Essential for: bones, teeth and kidneys.
Juicing it: celery, broccoli, melon, grapes, kiwi fruit, blackcurrants and milk.

Potassium

Essential for: nerves, brain health and kidney function; helps to lower blood pressure.
Juicing it: all fruits and vegetables.

Selenium

Essential for: liver and cardiovascular health.
Juicing it: Brazil nuts (richest source), green vegetables, garlic, onions, tomatoes and wheatgerm.

Sodium

Essential for: healthy nerve function; however, we tend to get too much of the sodium in our diet from salt, which contributes to high blood pressure and heart disease.
Juicing it: sodium is present in

ABOVE: *Drinks made from grapes and berries provide sulphur for healthy skin.*

small quantities in all fruit and vegetables, as well as seaweeds, and is balanced by potassium and water.

Sulphur

Essential for: healthy skin, hair and nails.
Juicing it: cabbage, garlic, onion, radish, cucumber, watercress, grapes and berries.

Zinc

Essential for: all protein metabolism, growth and healing, reproduction, immunity and digestion.
Juicing it: broccoli, cauliflower, carrots, cucumbers and raspberries are the best juicing sources of zinc; also try adding nuts and seeds, wheatgerm and brewer's yeast to juices and smoothies.

Index